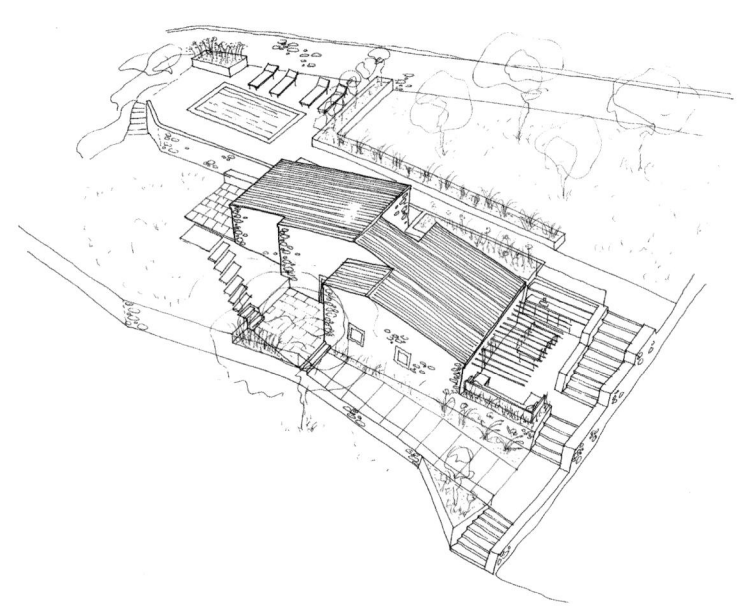

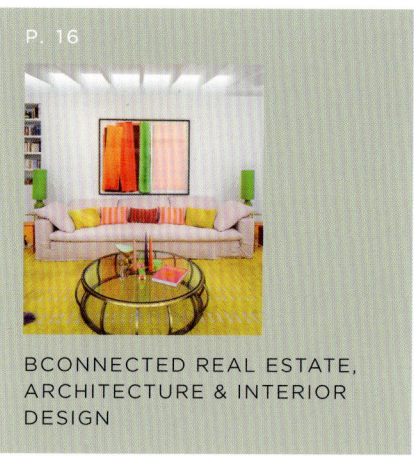

Architecture for Slow Living. Buildings where the landscape filters through the windows. Gardens designed for lingering. Spaces for casual chats and refuges for cooling off in the summer. In Mallorca, architecture is the backdrop to a lifestyle defined by the Mediterranean.

In this context, houses are natural extensions of the landscape. Whether in ancient homes renovated for modern life or new ones with essential volumes and minimalist spaces, tradition and avant-garde intertwine to tell a unique and fascinating story.

On this island, the largest of the Balearics, architecture is not mere construction, and design is not a showcase but a symbiosis between man and his environment, with spaces that invite contemplation and enjoyment. Every corner, every volume, every element dialogues with the topography, vegetation, and sea, shaping a unique aesthetic identity. The pages of this book reflect the work of a generation of architects, interior designers, and landscapers leaving their mark on an exceptional setting. Their works are spread across the island's geography. In the historic centers of cities, coves by the sea, the impressive landscapes of the Tramuntana mountains, and the stone villages of the rural interior, the houses, hotels, and gardens presented here shine with their own style and transcend with the Mediterranean spirit as a common banner.

Architektur für langsames Leben. Gebäude, in denen die Landschaft durch die Fenster hindurchscheint. Gärten, die zum Verweilen einladen. Orte für zwanglose Gespräche und Zufluchtsorte zum Abkühlen im Sommer. Auf Mallorca ist die Architektur der Hintergrund für einen Lebensstil, der vom Mittelmeer geprägt ist.

In diesem Kontext sind Häuser natürliche Erweiterungen der Landschaft. Ob in alten Häusern, die für das moderne Leben renoviert wurden, oder in neuen mit essentiellen Volumen und minimalistischen Räumen, Tradition und Avantgarde verschmelzen, um eine einzigartige und faszinierende Geschichte zu erzählen.

Auf dieser Insel, der größten der Balearen, ist Architektur nicht bloßes Bauen und Design keine Ausstellung, sondern eine Symbiose zwischen Mensch und Umwelt, mit Räumen, die zur Kontemplation und zum Genuss einladen. Jede Ecke, jedes Volumen, jedes Element steht im Dialog mit der Topographie, der Vegetation und dem Meer und formt eine einzigartige ästhetische Identität. Die Seiten dieses Buches spiegeln die Arbeit einer Generation von Architekten, Innenarchitekten und Landschaftsgestaltern wider, die ihre Spuren in einer außergewöhnlichen Umgebung hinterlassen. Ihre Werke sind über die gesamte Geografie der Insel verstreut. In den historischen Zentren der Städte, in Buchten am Meer, in den beeindruckenden Landschaften des Tramuntana-Gebirges und in den steinernen Dörfern des ländlichen Hinterlands erstrahlen die hier präsentierten Häuser, Hotels und Gärten mit eigenem Stil und tragen den mediterranen Geist als gemeinsames Banner.

Architecture pour une vie lente. Des bâtiments où le paysage filtre à travers les fenêtres. Des jardins conçus pour s'attarder. Des espaces pour des discussions informelles et des refuges pour se rafraîchir en été. À Majorque, l'architecture est le cadre d'un style de vie défini par la Méditerranée.

Dans ce contexte, les maisons sont des extensions naturelles du paysage. Qu'il s'agisse d'anciennes maisons rénovées pour la vie moderne ou de nouvelles avec des volumes essentiels et des espaces minimalistes, la tradition et l'avant-garde s'entrelacent pour raconter une histoire unique et fascinante.

Sur cette île, la plus grande des Baléares, l'architecture n'est pas une simple construction et le design n'est pas une vitrine, mais une symbiose entre l'homme et son environnement, avec des espaces qui invitent à la contemplation et au plaisir. Chaque coin, chaque volume, chaque élément dialogue avec la topographie, la végétation et la mer, façonnant une identité esthétique unique. Les pages de ce livre reflètent le travail d'une génération d'architectes, de designers d'intérieur et de paysagistes qui laissent leur empreinte dans un cadre exceptionnel. Leurs œuvres sont réparties à travers toute la géographie de l'île. Dans les centres historiques des villes, les criques en bord de mer, les paysages impressionnants de la Serra de Tramuntana et les villages de pierre de l'intérieur rural, les maisons, hôtels et jardins présentés ici brillent par leur style propre et transcendent avec l'esprit méditerranéen comme bannière commune.

Arquitectura para la vida lenta. Construcciones en las que se cuela el paisaje a través de las ventanas. Jardines pensados para transcurrir. Escenarios de charlas a la fresca y refugios para remojones durante el verano. En Mallorca, la arquitectura es escenario de un estilo de vida definido por el Mediterráneo.

En este contexto, las casas son extensiones naturales del paisaje. Ya sea en antiguas viviendas reformadas para la vida moderna, o nuevas con volúmenes esenciales y espacios minimalistas, la tradición y la vanguardia se entrelazan para contar una historia única y fascinante.

En esta isla, la más grande de las Baleares, la arquitectura no es mera construcción, y el diseño no es un escaparate, sino una simbiosis entre el hombre y su entorno, con espacios que invitan a la contemplación y el disfrute. Cada rincón, cada volumen, cada elemento, dialoga con la topografía, la vegetación y el mar, dando forma a una identidad estética propia. Las páginas de este libro reflejan la labor de una generación de arquitectos, interioristas y paisajistas que están dejando su huella en un escenario excepcional. Sus trabajos se reparten por toda la geografía de la isla. En los cascos históricos de las ciudades, las calas frente al mar, los impresionantes paisajes de la sierra de Tramuntana y los pueblos de piedra del interior rural, las casas, hoteles y jardines que aquí se presentan brillan por su estilo propio y trascienden con el espíritu mediterráneo como bandera común.

353 ARQUITECTES

FS HOME

ALARÓ

Photos © Xisco Kamal

This bright and open house was designed for a Dutch family seeking a home to enjoy the Mediterranean climate and improve their quality of life. This desire inspired an open and connected space configuration for this house that highlights the views from every perspective.

The house is built on a plot that was intended for an orchard. This land, with several descending terraces from the street access, offers impressive views of the old town. The house is oriented south to maximize light and views. On the ground floor are the kitchen, living-dining room, a porch, and the pool. Private areas like the garage, children's bedrooms, studio, and laundry are on the north side. The plot, with its descending topography and geometric shape without right angles, required careful volumetric design to make the most of the buildable space and comply with minimum setbacks. Dominated by materials like light-toned wood, iron, and stone, it integrates with the environment and evokes the old orchard terraces.

Dieses helle und offene Haus wurde für eine niederländische Familie entworfen, die ein Haus suchte, um das mediterrane Klima zu genießen und ihre Lebensqualität zu verbessern. Dieser Wunsch inspirierte eine Konfiguration offener und verbundener Räume für dieses Haus, das die Aussichten aus jeder Perspektive hervorhebt.

Das Haus ist auf einem Grundstück gebaut, das für einen Obstgarten vorgesehen war. Dieses Gelände, mit mehreren absteigenden Terrassen vom Straßenzugang, bietet beeindruckende Blicke auf die Altstadt. Das Haus ist nach Süden ausgerichtet, um Licht und Aussichten zu maximieren. Im Erdgeschoss befinden sich die Küche, das Wohn-Esszimmer, eine Veranda und der Pool. Private Bereiche wie die Garage, die Kinderzimmer, das Studio und die Waschküche befinden sich auf der Nordseite. Das Grundstück, mit seiner absteigenden Topographie und seiner geometrischen Form ohne rechte Winkel, erforderte ein sorgfältiges volumetrisches Design, um den bebaubaren Raum optimal zu nutzen und die Mindestabstände einzuhalten. Dominiert von Materialien wie hellem Holz, Eisen und Stein, integriert es sich in die Umgebung und erinnert an die alten Obstgarten-Terrassen.

Cette maison lumineuse et ouverte a été conçue pour une famille néerlandaise cherchant une maison pour profiter du climat méditerranéen et améliorer leur qualité de vie. Ce désir a inspiré une configuration d'espaces ouverts et connectés pour cette maison qui met en valeur les vues de chaque perspective.

La maison est construite sur un terrain destiné à un verger. Ce terrain, avec plusieurs terrasses descendant depuis l'accès de la rue, offre des vues impressionnantes sur la vieille ville. La maison est orientée au sud pour maximiser la lumière et les vues. Au rez-de-chaussée se trouvent la cuisine, le salon-salle à manger, un porche et la piscine. Les zones privées comme le garage, les chambres des enfants, le studio et la buanderie sont situées au nord. Le terrain, avec sa topographie descendante et sa forme géométrique sans angles droits, a nécessité une conception volumétrique soignée pour tirer le meilleur parti de l'espace constructible et respecter les reculs minimaux. Dominée par des matériaux comme le bois clair, le fer et la pierre, elle s'intègre à l'environnement et évoque les anciennes terrasses du verger.

Esta casa luminosa y abierta al exterior ha sido diseñada para una familia holandesa que buscaba un hogar donde disfrutar del clima mediterráneo y mejorar su calidad de vida. Este deseo inspiró una configuración de espacios abiertos y conectados para esta vivienda, que resalta las vistas desde cualquier perspectiva.

La casa está construida en un solar que estaba destinado a un huerto. Este terreno, con varios bancales descendentes desde el acceso de la calle, ofrece vistas impresionantes hacia el casco antiguo del pueblo. La casa se orienta al sur para maximizar la luz y las vistas. En la planta baja están la cocina, el salón comedor, un porche y la piscina. Las áreas privadas como el garaje, los dormitorios infantiles, el estudio y el lavadero están al norte. El terreno, con su topografía descendente y forma geométrica sin ángulos rectos, requirió un diseño volumétrico cuidadoso para aprovechar al máximo el espacio edificable y cumplir con los retranqueos mínimos. Dominan los materiales como la madera en tonos claros, hierro y piedra, integrándose con el entorno y evocando los antiguos bancales del huerto.

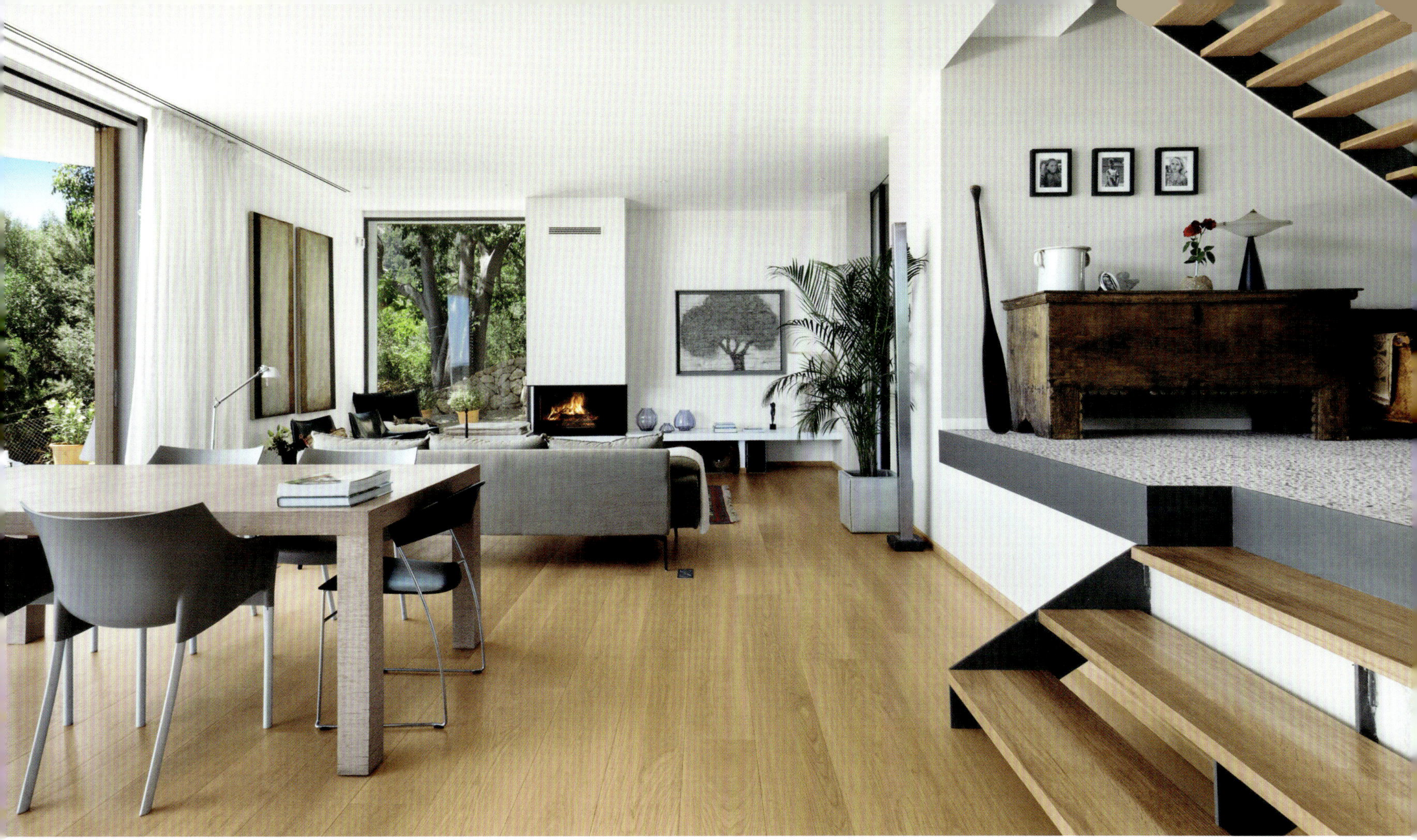

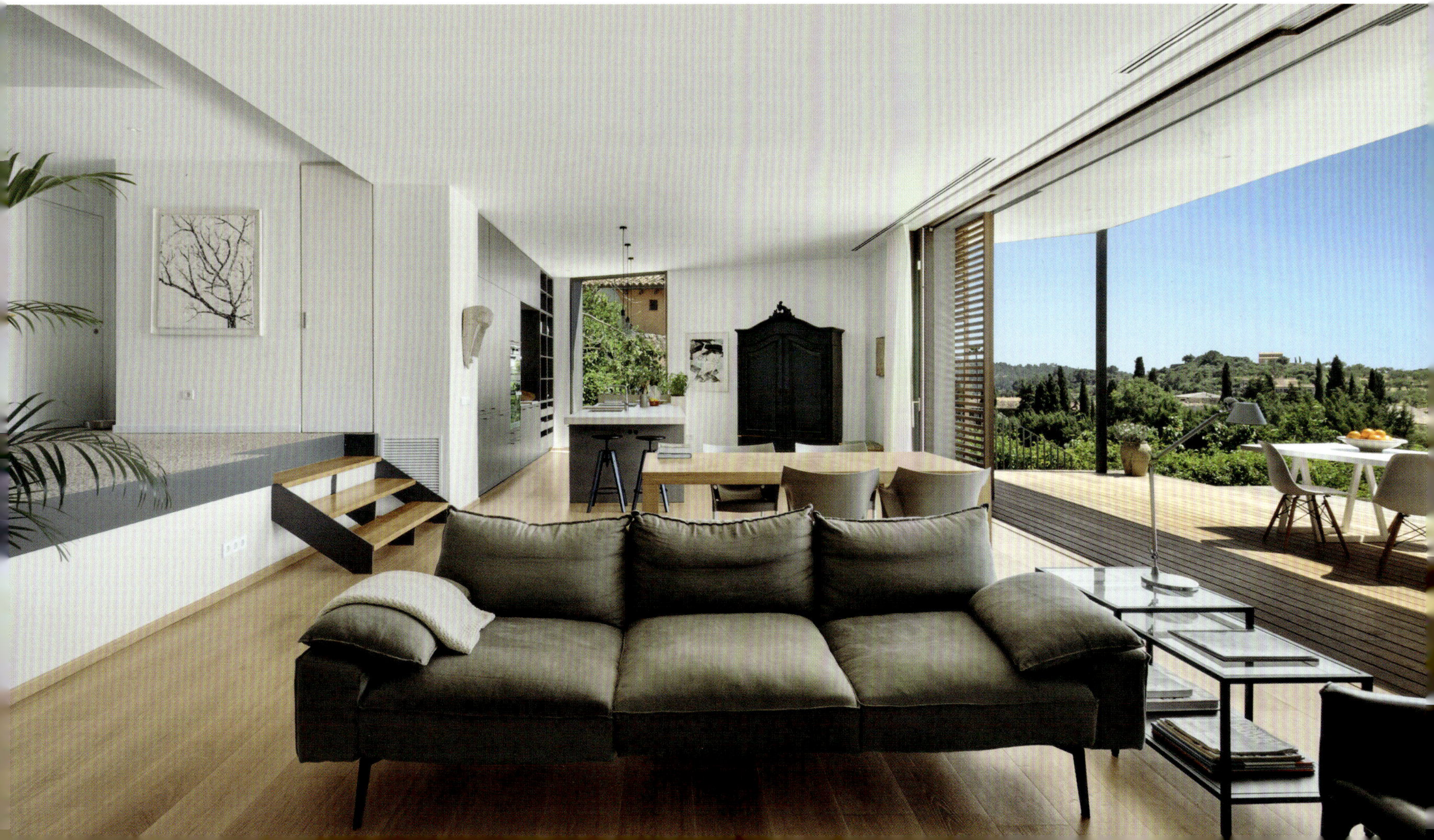

AN OPEN LAYOUT HIGHLIGHTS THE VIEWS
FROM ALL PERSPECTIVES

BCONNECTED
REAL ESTATE,
ARCHITECTURE &
INTERIOR DESIGN

SAT CHIT ANANDA

PALMA DE MALLORCA

Photos © bconnected

"Sat Chit Ananda" is a property surrounded by fields and almond trees, with the gentle tinkling of sheep bells as a backdrop. This retreat, located in the rolling hills of Mallorca, 10 kilometers from Palma, stands as an oasis of creativity and design. The main house is the epicenter of the estate and an ode to artistic freedom and the bold fusion of tradition and modernity. Inside, handmade rugs coexist with vibrantly colored door handles, a pink kitchen, and artworks that blend with furniture designed expressly for this space. Each room is a feast of colors and a sensory experience reflecting the distinctive signature of Christine Leja. The adjacent guest house, with its own colorful style, invites prolonged stays and is complemented by a space for an independent creative studio. The property is surrounded by a Mediterranean garden that extends on two levels and merges with the stunning landscape. What was once an old estate is now a place of inspiration and well-being where past and future interact in perfect harmony. More than a simple dwelling, "Sat Chit Ananda" represents a lifestyle.

„Sat Chit Ananda" ist ein Anwesen, umgeben von Feldern und Mandelbäumen, mit dem sanften Klingeln der Schafsglocken im Hintergrund. Dieses Refugium, gelegen in den sanften Hügeln von Mallorca, 10 Kilometer von Palma entfernt, präsentiert sich als Oase der Kreativität und des Designs. Das Haupthaus ist das Epizentrum des Anwesens und eine Ode an die künstlerische Freiheit sowie die mutige Verschmelzung von Tradition und Moderne. Im Inneren koexistieren handgefertigte Teppiche mit leuchtend bunten Türgriffen, einer rosa Küche und Kunstwerken, die sich mit speziell für diesen Raum entworfenen Möbeln vermischen. Jeder Raum ist ein Fest der Farben und eine sensorische Erfahrung, die die unverwechselbare Handschrift von Christine Leja widerspiegelt. Das angrenzende Gästehaus, mit eigenem bunten Stil, lädt zu längeren Aufenthalten ein und wird durch einen Raum für ein unabhängiges kreatives Studio ergänzt. Das Anwesen ist von einem mediterranen Garten umgeben, der sich auf zwei Ebenen erstreckt und sich nahtlos in die beeindruckende Landschaft einfügt. Was einst ein altes Anwesen war, ist heute ein Ort der Inspiration und des Wohlbefindens, wo Vergangenheit und Zukunft in perfekter Harmonie interagieren. Mehr als nur ein einfaches Wohnhaus, repräsentiert „Sat Chit Ananda" einen Lebensstil.

« Sat Chit Ananda » est une propriété entourée de champs et d'amandiers, avec le doux tintement des clochettes des moutons en toile de fond. Ce refuge, situé dans les collines ondulantes de Majorque, à 10 kilomètres de Palma, se présente comme un oasis de créativité et de design. La maison principale est l'épicentre de la propriété et une ode à la liberté artistique et à l'audacieuse fusion de la tradition et de la modernité. À l'intérieur, des tapis faits à la main cohabitent avec des poignées de portes de couleur vive, une cuisine rose et des œuvres d'art qui se fondent avec des meubles conçus spécialement pour cet espace. Chaque pièce est un festin de couleurs et une expérience sensorielle reflétant la signature distinctive de Christine Leja. La maison d'hôtes adjacente, avec son propre style coloré, invite à des séjours prolongés et est complétée par un espace pour un studio créatif indépendant. La propriété est entourée d'un jardin méditerranéen qui s'étend sur deux niveaux et se fond avec le paysage impressionnant. Ce qui était autrefois un ancien domaine est aujourd'hui un lieu d'inspiration et de bien-être où le passé et le futur interagissent en parfaite harmonie. Plus qu'une simple demeure, « Sat Chit Ananda » représente un style de vie.

«Sat Chit Ananda» es una propiedad rodeada de campos y almendros con el suave tintineo de los cencerros de las ovejas como telón de fondo. Este refugio situado en las colinas ondulantes de Mallorca, a 10 km de Palma, se erige como un oasis de creatividad y diseño. La casa principal es el epicentro de la finca, una oda a la libertad artística y la audaz fusión de tradición y modernidad. En su interior, alfombras hechas a mano conviven con manillas de puertas de vibrante color amarillo, una cocina rosa y obras de arte que se integran con muebles diseñados expresamente para este espacio. Cada habitación es un festín de colores y una experiencia sensorial, reflejando la distintiva firma de Christine Leja. La casa de invitados adyacente, con su propio estilo colorido, invita a la estancia prolongada y se complementa con un espacio para un estudio creativo independiente. La propiedad está rodeada de un jardín mediterráneo que se extiende en dos niveles y se funde con el impresionante paisaje. Lo que alguna vez fue una vieja finca, hoy es un lugar de inspiración y bienestar donde pasado y futuro interactúan en perfecta armonía. Más que una simple vivienda, «Sat Chit Ananda» representa un estilo de vida.

EACH ROOM IS A FEAST OF COLORS
AND A SENSORY EXPERIENCE, REFLECTING THE
DISTINCTIVE SIGNATURE OF CHRISTINE LEJA

CARLOS SERRA
INTERIORISMO

HOTEL BAREFOOT

PORTOCOLOM

Photos © Luis Beltrán

Portocolom, a picturesque fishing village with the largest natural harbor in Mallorca, is the setting for this hotel oriented towards rest and relaxation, dominated by earth tones, craftsmanship, and natural textures. A handmade glazed clay counter and artisanal lamps welcome guests in the reception area. The spacious entrance hall with sofas and water hyacinth armchairs next to a built-in bookshelf and an impressive vinyl panel of golden dunes exudes peace and harmony. The artisanal tone continues in the rooms with handmade macramé headboards and natural colors. Bathrooms with stone benches and showers covered in handcrafted glazed tiles complement the concept.

The heart of the hotel is the central pool built with Marés stone and surrounded by a large esplanade with hammocks and a chill-out area. The spa, which also uses this stone in its finishes, offers a hammam, a sauna, and massage cabins. Private terraces with abundant vegetation and spiral staircases feature relaxation beds and jacuzzis to complete this oasis of tranquility and rest.

Portocolom, ein malerisches Fischerdorf mit dem größten Naturhafen Mallorcas, ist der Schauplatz dieses Hotels, das auf Ruhe und Entspannung ausgerichtet ist und von Erdtönen, Handwerkskunst und natürlichen Texturen dominiert wird. Eine handgefertigte Theke aus glasiertem Ton und handgefertigte Lampen empfangen die Gäste im Empfangsbereich. Die geräumige Eingangshalle mit Sofas und Wasserhyazinthen-Stühlen neben einem eingebauten Bücherregal und einem beeindruckenden Vinyl-Panel mit goldenen Dünen strahlt Frieden und Harmonie aus. Der handwerkliche Ton setzt sich in den Zimmern mit handgefertigten Makramee-Kopfenden und natürlichen Farben fort. Badezimmer mit Steinbänken und Duschen, die mit handgefertigten glasierten Fliesen verkleidet sind, ergänzen das Konzept.

Das Herzstück des Hotels ist der zentrale Pool, der mit marés-Stein gebaut und von einer großen Esplanade mit Hängematten und einer Chill-Out-Zone umgeben ist. Das Spa, das ebenfalls diesen Stein in seinen Oberflächen verwendet, bietet ein Hammam, eine Sauna und Massageräume. Private Terrassen mit reichlich Vegetation und Wendeltreppen verfügen über Entspannungsbetten und Whirlpools, um dieses Refugium der Ruhe und Erholung zu vervollständigen.

Portocolom, un pittoresque village de pêcheurs avec le plus grand port naturel de Majorque, est le cadre de cet hôtel orienté vers le repos et la détente, dominé par des tons terre, l'artisanat et des textures naturelles. Un comptoir en argile émaillée à la main et des lampes artisanales accueillent les invités à la réception. Le vaste hall d'entrée avec des canapés et des fauteuils en jacinthe d'eau à côté d'une bibliothèque intégrée et d'un impressionnant panneau en vinyle de dunes dorées exhale paix et harmonie. Le ton artisanal se poursuit dans les chambres avec des têtes de lit en macramé faites à la main et des couleurs naturelles. Les salles de bains avec des bancs en pierre et des douches revêtues de carreaux émaillés à la main complètent le concept.

Le cœur de l'hôtel est la piscine centrale construite en pierre de marés et entourée d'une vaste esplanade avec des hamacs et une zone de détente. Le spa, qui utilise également cette pierre dans ses finitions, propose un hammam, un sauna et des cabines de massage. Les terrasses privées avec une végétation abondante et des escaliers en colimaçon sont dotées de lits de relaxation et de jacuzzis pour compléter cet oasis de tranquillité et de repos.

Portocolom, un pintoresco pueblo de pescadores con el puerto natural más grande de Mallorca, es escenario de este hotel orientado al descanso y la relajación, en el que dominan los colores tierra, la artesanía y las texturas naturales. Un mostrador de barro esmaltado a mano y lámparas artesanales, da la bienvenida en la recepción. El amplio hall de entrada, con sofás y sillones de jacinto acuático, junto a una estantería de obra y un impresionante panel vinílico de dunas doradas, transmite paz y armonía. El tono artesanal continúa en las habitaciones con cabezales de macramé hechos a mano, y colores naturales. Los baños, con bancadas de piedra y duchas revestidas de azulejos de barro esmaltados artesanalmente, complementan el concepto.

El corazón del hotel es la piscina central, construida con piedra de Marés y rodeada por una amplia explanada con hamacas y una zona de chill out. El spa, que también utiliza esta piedra en sus acabados, ofrece un hammam, una sauna y cabinas de masaje. Las terrazas privadas con vegetación abundante y escaleras de caracol cuentan con camas de relax y jacuzzis, para completar este oasis de tranquilidad y descanso.

EARTH TONES, CRAFTSMANSHIP AND NATURAL TEXTURES
APPEAL TO CALM AND RELAXATION

CMV ARCHITECTS

SOL DE MALLORCA

CALVIÀ

Photos © Tomeu Canyelles

Located on a large corner plot, this L-shaped single-family house with a lush garden as a central element has been conceived as an oasis of tranquility where the boundaries between indoor and outdoor blur. The design studio of Thomas Griem (TG Studio) commissioned the construction to CMV Architects and collaborated on the interior design.

The 470 m² building is mainly distributed on the ground floor with large sliding carpentries that hide in the walls, creating a seamless transition between the interior and the garden. The upper floor houses the main bedroom with stunning views of the Bay of Palma. Interior finishes highlight the use of natural materials such as Mallorcan stone and local wood. The entrance, marked by a corten steel door, leads to a spacious open-plan living-dining area and kitchen with high ceilings where clean lines and modern furniture prevail. An outdoor dining area with a wooden terrace surrounded by grass is the spot for long meals. The garden designed by landscaper Stephen Woodhams features palm trees and olive trees, integrating as part of the house for much of the year.

Auf einem großen Eckgrundstück gelegen, wurde dieses L-förmige Einfamilienhaus mit einem üppigen Garten als zentrales Element als Oase der Ruhe konzipiert, in der die Grenzen zwischen Innen und Außen verschwimmen. Das Designstudio von Thomas Griem (TG Studio) beauftragte den Bau bei CMV Architects und arbeitete an der Innenausstattung mit.

Das 470 m² große Gebäude ist hauptsächlich auf das Erdgeschoss verteilt, mit großen Schiebefenstern, die in den Wänden verschwinden und so einen nahtlosen Übergang zwischen dem Inneren und dem Garten schaffen. Das obere Stockwerk beherbergt das Hauptschlafzimmer mit atemberaubendem Blick auf die Bucht von Palma. Die Innenausstattung betont die Verwendung natürlicher Materialien wie mallorquinischen Stein und lokales Holz. Der Eingang, markiert durch eine Cortenstahl-Tür, führt zu einem geräumigen offenen Wohn-Essbereich und einer Küche mit hohen Decken, in denen klare Linien und moderne Möbel vorherrschen. Ein Essbereich im Freien mit einer Holzterrasse, umgeben von Gras, ist der Ort für lange Mahlzeiten. Der von Landschaftsgestalter Stephen Woodhams gestaltete Garten verfügt über Palmen und Olivenbäume und integriert sich über einen Großteil des Jahres als Teil des Hauses.

Située sur un grand terrain d'angle, cette maison unifamiliale en forme de L avec un jardin luxuriant comme élément central a été conçue comme un oasis de tranquillité où les frontières entre intérieur et extérieur se confondent. Le studio de design de Thomas Griem (TG Studio) a commandé la construction à CMV Architects et a collaboré sur la conception intérieure.

Le bâtiment de 470 m² est principalement réparti sur le rez-de-chaussée avec de grandes menuiseries coulissantes qui se cachent dans les murs, créant une transition fluide entre l'intérieur et le jardin. L'étage supérieur abrite la chambre principale avec des vues époustouflantes sur la baie de Palma. Les finitions intérieures mettent en valeur l'utilisation de matériaux naturels tels que la pierre majorquine et le bois local. L'entrée, marquée par une porte en acier corten, mène à un vaste espace de vie ouvert avec des plafonds hauts où prédominent des lignes épurées et des meubles modernes. Une salle à manger en plein air avec une terrasse en bois entourée de pelouse est l'endroit idéal pour de longs repas. Le jardin conçu par le paysagiste Stephen Woodhams comporte des palmiers et des oliviers, s'intégrant comme partie de la maison pendant une grande partie de l'année.

Ubicada en un amplio solar de esquina, esta vivienda unifamiliar en forma de L y un exuberante jardín como elemento central, ha sido concebida como un oasis de tranquilidad, donde los límites entre interior y exterior se desdibujan. El estudio de diseño de Thomas Griem (TG Studio) encargó la construcción a CMV Architects y colaboró en el diseño de interiores.

La edificación de 470 m² se distribuye principalmente en planta baja, con grandes carpinterías correderas que se ocultan en los muros, creando una transición fluida entre el interior y el jardín. La planta superior alberga la habitación principal, con vistas deslumbrantes a la bahía de Palma. Los acabados interiores destacan por el uso de materiales naturales, como la piedra mallorquina y la madera local. La entrada, marcada por una puerta de acero corten, da paso a un amplio espacio de estar, comedor y cocina de planta abierta con techos altos, donde predominan líneas limpias y muebles de diseño moderno. Un comedor al aire libre, con una terraza de madera y rodeado de césped, es la zona para disfrutar de largas comidas. El jardín, diseñado por el paisajista Stephen Woodhams, cuenta con palmeras y olivos, integrándose como parte de la vivienda durante gran parte del año.

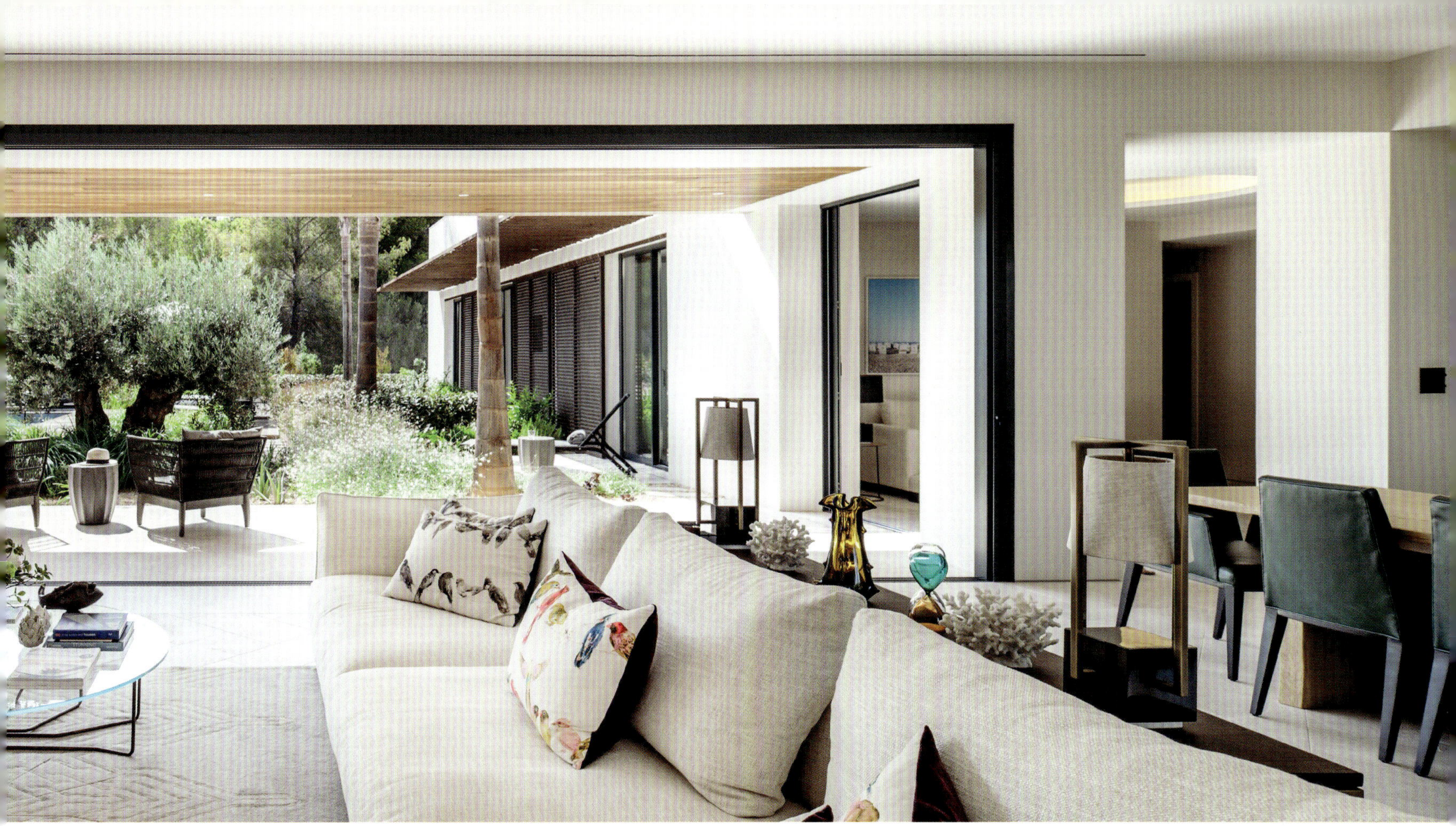

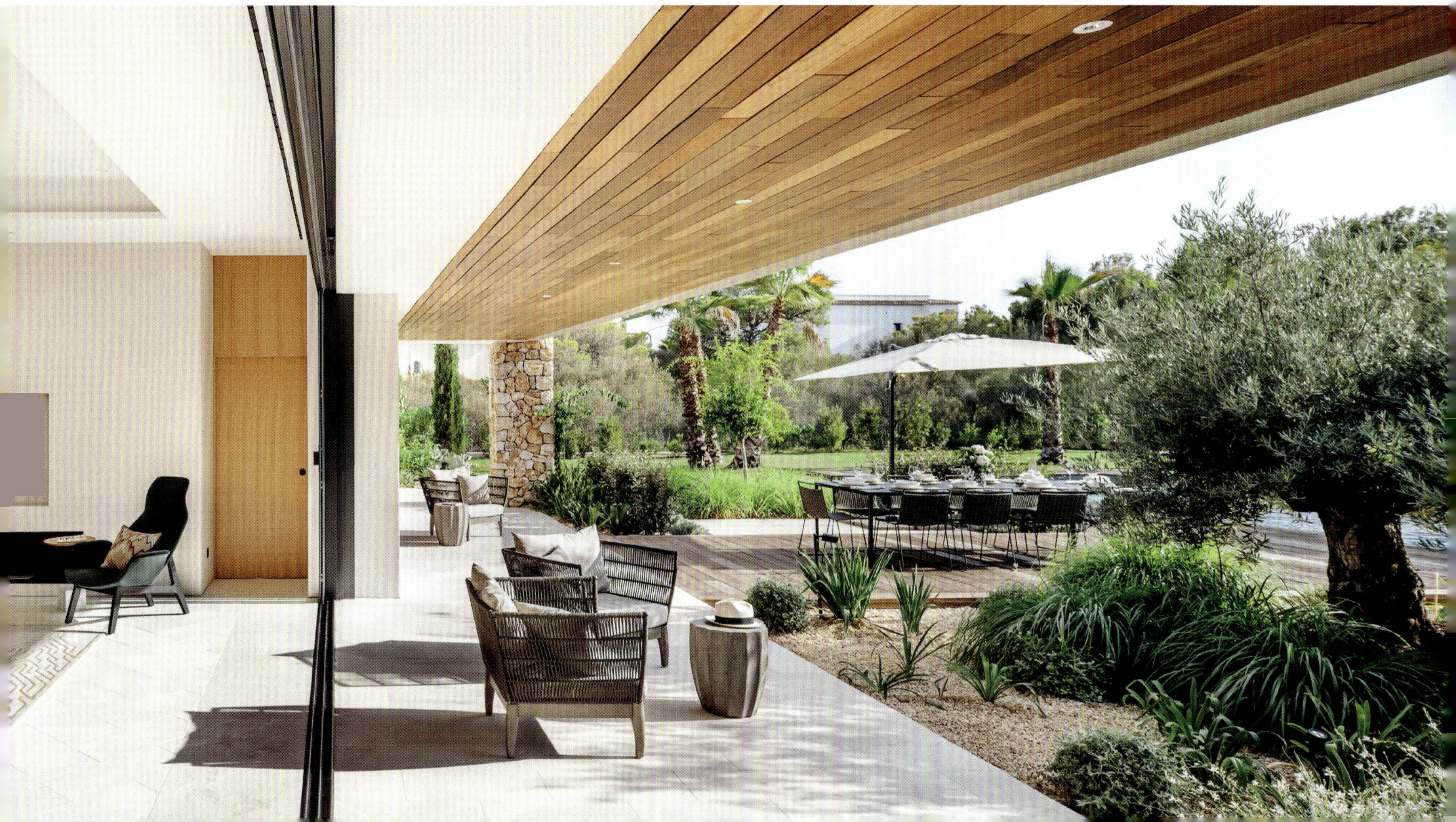

THE HOUSE SEAMLESSLY CONNECTS
THE INTERIOR WITH THE GARDEN

DOMUM PROJECTS

BN1 HOUSE

PALMA DE MALLORCA

Photos © Tomeu Canyellas

This family house is determined by an unconventional layout that maximizes natural light and the scenic surroundings of the terrain. Located in the quiet residential area of Son Vida, the two-story house has an unusual arrangement: the bedrooms are on the lower floor, while the common areas and pool terrace are on the upper level, offering the best panoramic views. In this DOMUM PROJECTS house, natural materials such as stone and wood dominate, providing uniformity and visual cohesion. The lower floor enjoys abundant natural light and a double-height space. The staircase with a metal structure clad in wood and a lacquered white railing connects both levels. The upper floor is an open space that integrates the living-dining room and kitchen with a central island that allows cooking while enjoying views of the pool. Sliding windows three meters high, hidden in Iroko volumes, connect the interior with the exterior. The exterior pavement changes from stone to wooden decking around the pool, which is clad in dark green mosaic and features a shallow area for children.

Dieses Familienhaus zeichnet sich durch eine unkonventionelle Anordnung aus, die das natürliche Licht und die landschaftlichen Umgebungen des Geländes maximiert. In der ruhigen Wohngegend von Son Vida gelegen, hat das zweistöckige Haus eine ungewöhnliche Anordnung: Die Schlafzimmer befinden sich im unteren Stockwerk, während die Gemeinschaftsräume und die Poolterrasse im oberen Stockwerk sind, um die besten Panoramablicke zu bieten. Bei diesem Projekt von DOMUM PROJECTS dominieren natürliche Materialien wie Stein und Holz, die für Einheitlichkeit und optischen Zusammenhalt sorgen. Das untere Stockwerk genießt reichlich natürliches Licht und einen doppelstöckigen Raum. Die Treppe mit einer Metallstruktur, die mit Holz verkleidet und mit einem weiß lackierten Geländer versehen ist, verbindet beide Ebenen. Das obere Stockwerk ist ein offener Raum, der Wohnzimmer, Esszimmer und Küche mit einer zentralen Insel integriert, die das Kochen ermöglicht und gleichzeitig die Aussicht auf den Pool genießt. Drei Meter hohe Schiebefenster, die in iroko-Volumen verborgen sind, verbinden das Innere mit dem Äußeren. Der Außenbelag wechselt von Stein zu Holzterrassen rund um den Pool, der mit dunkelgrünem Mosaik verkleidet ist und einen flachen Bereich für Kinder bietet.

Cette maison familiale se caractérise par une disposition non conventionnelle qui maximise la lumière naturelle et les paysages environnants du terrain. Située dans la paisible zone résidentielle de Son Vida, la maison de deux étages a une disposition inhabituelle : les chambres se trouvent à l'étage inférieur tandis que les espaces communs et la terrasse de la piscine sont à l'étage supérieur, offrant ainsi les meilleures vues panoramiques. Dans cette maison du DOMUM PROJECTS les matériaux naturels tels que la pierre et le bois dominent, apportant uniformité et cohésion visuelle. L'étage inférieur bénéficie d'une abondante lumière naturelle et d'un espace à double hauteur. L'escalier avec une structure métallique revêtue de bois et une balustrade laquée en blanc relie les deux niveaux. L'étage supérieur est un espace ouvert intégrant salon, salle à manger et cuisine avec une île centrale permettant de cuisiner tout en profitant des vues sur la piscine. Les fenêtres coulissantes de trois mètres de haut, dissimulées dans des volumes en iroko, relient l'intérieur à l'extérieur. Le revêtement de sol extérieur passe de la pierre à la terrasse en bois autour de la piscine, qui est revêtue de mosaïque vert foncé et dispose d'une zone peu profonde pour les enfants.

Esta casa familiar se caracteriza por una distribución poco convencional que maximiza la luz natural y el entorno escénico del terreno. Ubicada en la tranquila área residencial de Son Vida, la vivienda de dos plantas tiene una disposición inusual: las habitaciones se encuentran en la planta inferior, mientras que las áreas comunes y la terraza de la piscina están en el nivel superior, ofreciendo así las mejores vistas panorámicas. En esta casa de DOMUM PROJECTS dominan los materiales naturales como la piedra y la madera, que aportan uniformidad y cohesión visual. La planta inferior disfruta de abundante luz natural y un espacio a doble altura. La escalera, con estructura metálica revestida en madera y barandilla lacada en blanco, conecta ambos niveles. La planta superior es un espacio diáfano que integra salón, comedor y cocina con isla central que permite cocinar mientras se disfruta de las vistas hacia la piscina. Los ventanales correderos de tres metros de altura, ocultos en volúmenes de iroko, conectan el interior con el exterior. El pavimento exterior cambia de piedra a tarima de madera alrededor de la piscina, que está revestida en mosaico verde oscuro y cuenta con una zona de poca profundidad para niños.

Ground floor plan

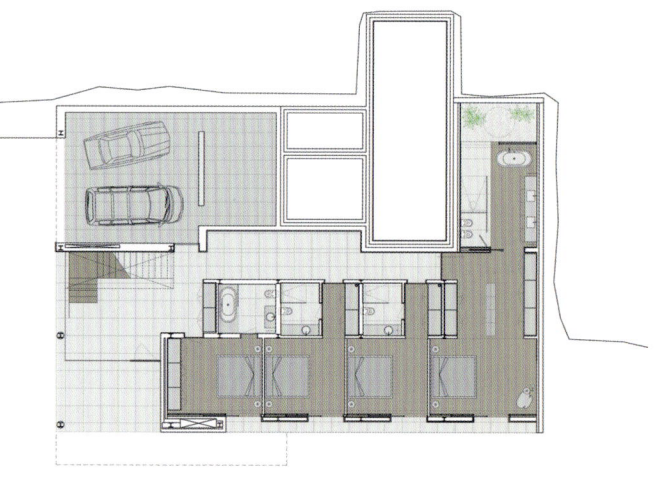

First floor plan

NATURAL STONE AND WOOD DOMINATE, ENSURING
UNIFORMITY AND VISUAL COHESION

GINARD LUETHJE WOLF – ARCHITECTS & DESIGNERS

CASA ORIENT

PORTOPETRO

Photos © Bernd Kusber, Javier Catalá

CALA EGOS

SANTANYI

Photos © Santiago Stankovic

Located in the southeast of Mallorca, this modern villa standing on gently sloping terrain has an imposing and elegant presence. The architect´s design has been oriented in all its aspects to ensure the house harmoniously integrates with the surrounding landscape. The structure of this house merges traditional and modern elements, incorporating characteristic features of Mallorcan architectural culture such as shutters and stone walls. The transparency and the way interior and exterior spaces are articulated are the central pillars of the design. This created wide-open and light-filled spaces.

The sun-drenched plot offers panoramic views of the Mediterranean landscape. The south terrace and pool are strategically located at this level, providing an oasis of relaxation and recreation. The patio with an olive tree offers privacy and connection with nature. A balcony suspended between the building structures provides shade on the hottest summer days, lightness, and a visual link to the blue sea on the horizon.

Im Südosten von Mallorca gelegen, erhebt sich diese moderne Villa auf sanft abfallendem Gelände und hat eine imposante und elegante Präsenz. Das Design wurde in all seinen Aspekten so ausgerichtet, dass das Haus harmonisch in die umgebende Landschaft integriert ist. Die Struktur dieses Hauses verbindet traditionelle und moderne Elemente und integriert charakteristische Merkmale der mallorquinischen Baukultur wie Fensterläden und Steinmauern. Die Transparenz und die Art und Weise, wie Innen- und Außenräume miteinander verbunden sind, sind die zentralen Säulen des Designs. So wurden weitläufige, offene und lichtdurchflutete Räume geschaffen.

Das sonnendurchflutete Grundstück bietet Panoramablicke auf die mediterrane Landschaft. Die Südterrasse und der Pool sind strategisch auf dieser Ebene gelegen und bieten ein Refugium der Entspannung und Freizeit. Der Innenhof mit einem Olivenbaum bietet Privatsphäre und Verbindung zur Natur. Ein zwischen den Gebäudestrukturen schwebender Balkon bietet an den heißesten Sommertagen Schatten, Leichtigkeit und eine visuelle Verbindung zum blauen Meer am Horizont.

Située dans le sud-est de Majorque, cette villa moderne, s'élevant sur un terrain en pente douce, a une présence imposante et élégante. Le design a été orienté dans tous ses aspects pour que la maison s'intègre harmonieusement avec le paysage environnant. La structure de cette maison fusionne des éléments traditionnels et modernes, incorporant des caractéristiques de la culture architecturale majorquine comme les volets et les murs en pierre. La transparence et la manière dont les espaces intérieurs et extérieurs sont articulés sont les piliers centraux du design. Ainsi, de vastes espaces ouverts et lumineux ont été créés.

La parcelle baignée de soleil offre des vues panoramiques sur le paysage méditerranéen. La terrasse sud et la piscine sont stratégiquement situées à ce niveau, offrant un oasis de détente et de loisirs. Le patio avec un olivier offre intimité et connexion avec la nature. Un balcon suspendu entre les structures du bâtiment fournit de l'ombre lors des journées les plus chaudes de l'été, de la légèreté et un lien visuel avec la mer bleue à l'horizon.

Situada en el sureste de Mallorca, esta villa moderna que se levanta sobre un terreno de suave pendiente tiene una presencia imponente y elegante. El diseño, se ha orientado en todos sus aspectos para que la casa se integre de manera armónica con el paisaje circundante. La estructura de esta vivienda fusiona lo tradicional y lo moderno, incorporando elementos característicos de la cultura arquitectónica mallorquina, como las persianas y los muros de piedra. La transparencia y la manera en cómo se articulan los espacios interiores y exteriores son los pilares centrales del diseño. De esta manera se generaron amplios espacios abiertos y llenos de luz.

La parcela, bañada por el sol, ofrece vistas panorámicas del paisaje mediterráneo. La terraza sur y la piscina se sitúan estratégicamente en este nivel, proporcionando un oasis de relajación y esparcimiento. El patio con un olivo brinda intimidad y conexión con la naturaleza. Un balcón suspendido entre las estructuras del edificio ofrece sombra en los días más intensos del verano, ligereza y un vínculo visual con el mar azul en el horizonte.

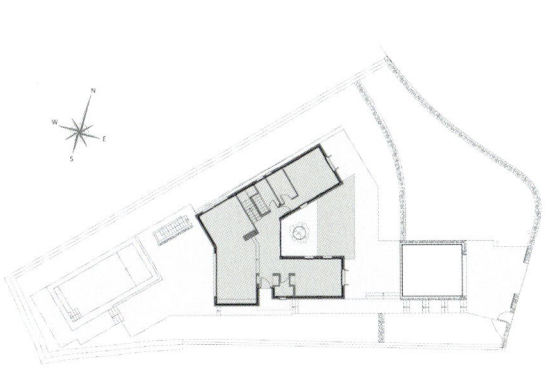

Site plan

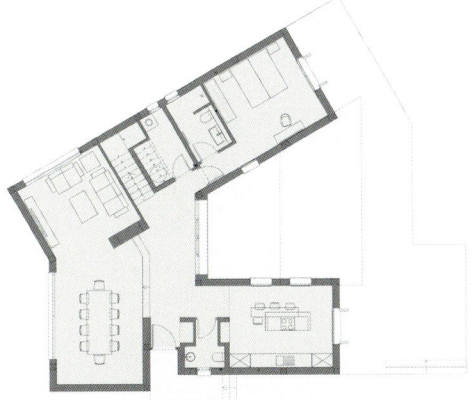

Ground floor plan

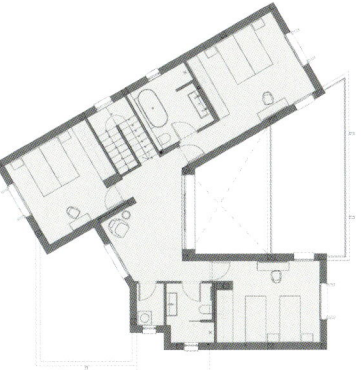

First floor plan

THE DESIGN FOCUSES ON TRANSPARENCY AND
SEAMLESS INDOOR-OUTDOOR SPACES

Elegant and sustainable, this contemporary residence integrates into the landscape and boasts spectacular sea views. The design by the team of architects is oriented towards maximum comfort and family enjoyment, with transitional spaces providing privacy and a large porch regulating sunlight and providing shade year-round. The building is strategically oriented to maximize panoramic views. Its design presents an interesting duality: the public façade shows staggered and fragmented volumes, while the private area facing the pool exhibits marked horizontality contrasted by the verticality of a stone cube. The fluid layout connects indoor and outdoor spaces, all oriented towards the sea. The house is energy-efficient, leveraging passive ventilation and lighting-thermal control systems. The insulated envelope, carpentry, and combination of renewable energies enhance its sustainability.

Elegant und nachhaltig integriert sich diese zeitgenössische Residenz in die Landschaft und bietet spektakuläre Ausblicke auf das Meer. Das Design des Architektenteams ist auf maximalen Komfort und Familiengenuss ausgerichtet, mit Übergangsräumen, die Privatsphäre bieten und einem großen Veranda, die das Sonnenlicht reguliert und das ganze Jahr über Schatten spendet. Das Gebäude ist strategisch ausgerichtet, um Panoramablicke zu maximieren. Sein Design präsentiert eine interessante Dualität: Die öffentliche Fassade zeigt gestaffelte und fragmentierte Volumen, während der private Bereich zum Pool hin eine ausgeprägte Horizontalität aufweist, die durch die Vertikalität eines Steinkubus kontrastiert wird. Die fließende Anordnung verbindet Innen- und Außenräume, die alle auf das Meer ausgerichtet sind. Das Haus ist energieeffizient und nutzt passive Belüftungs- und Lichtthermokontrollsysteme. Die isolierte Hülle, die Tischlerei und die Kombination erneuerbarer Energien erhöhen die Nachhaltigkeit.

Élégante et durable, cette résidence contemporaine s'intègre dans le paysage et offre des vues spectaculaires sur la mer. Le design de l'équipe d'architectes est orienté vers le confort maximal et le plaisir familial, avec des espaces de transition offrant intimité et un grand porche régulant l'entrée de la lumière solaire et apportant de l'ombre toute l'année. Le bâtiment est orienté de manière stratégique pour maximiser les vues panoramiques. Son design présente une dualité intéressante : la façade publique montre des volumes étagés et fragmentés, tandis que la zone privée donnant sur la piscine exhibe une horizontalité marquée contrastée par la verticalité d'un cube de pierre. La disposition fluide connecte les espaces intérieurs et extérieurs, tous orientés vers la mer. La maison est économe en énergie, exploitant des systèmes de ventilation passive et de contrôle thermo-lumineux. L'enveloppe isolée, les menuiseries et la combinaison d'énergies renouvelables renforcent sa durabilité.

Elegante y sostenible, esta residencia contemporánea se integra al paisaje y cuenta con unas vistas espectaculares al mar. El diseño del equipo de arquitectos está orientado a la máxima comodidad y el disfrute familiar. Incluye espacios de transición que proporcionan privacidad y un gran porche que regula la entrada de luz solar y aporta sombra durante todo el año. El edificio está orientado de manera estratégica para maximizar las vistas panorámicas. Su diseño presenta una dualidad interesante: la fachada pública muestra volúmenes escalonados y fragmentados, mientras que la zona privada que da hacia la piscina, exhibe una marcada horizontalidad, contrastada por la verticalidad de un cubo de piedra. La distribución fluida conecta los espacios interiores y exteriores, todos orientados hacia el mar. La casa es energéticamente eficiente, aprovechando sistemas pasivos de ventilación y control lumínico-térmico. La envolvente aislada, las carpinterías y la combinación de energías renovables refuerzan su sostenibilidad.

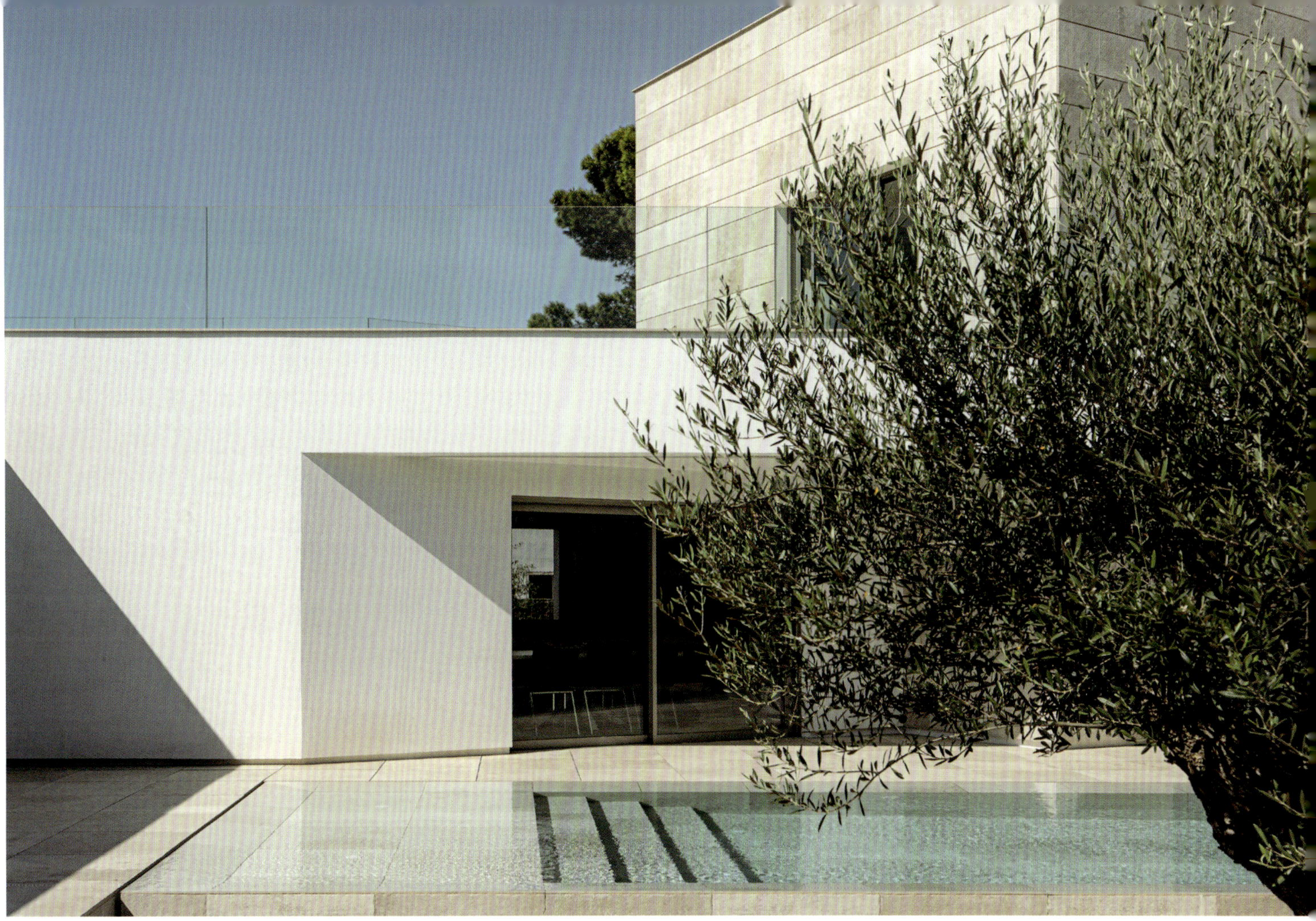
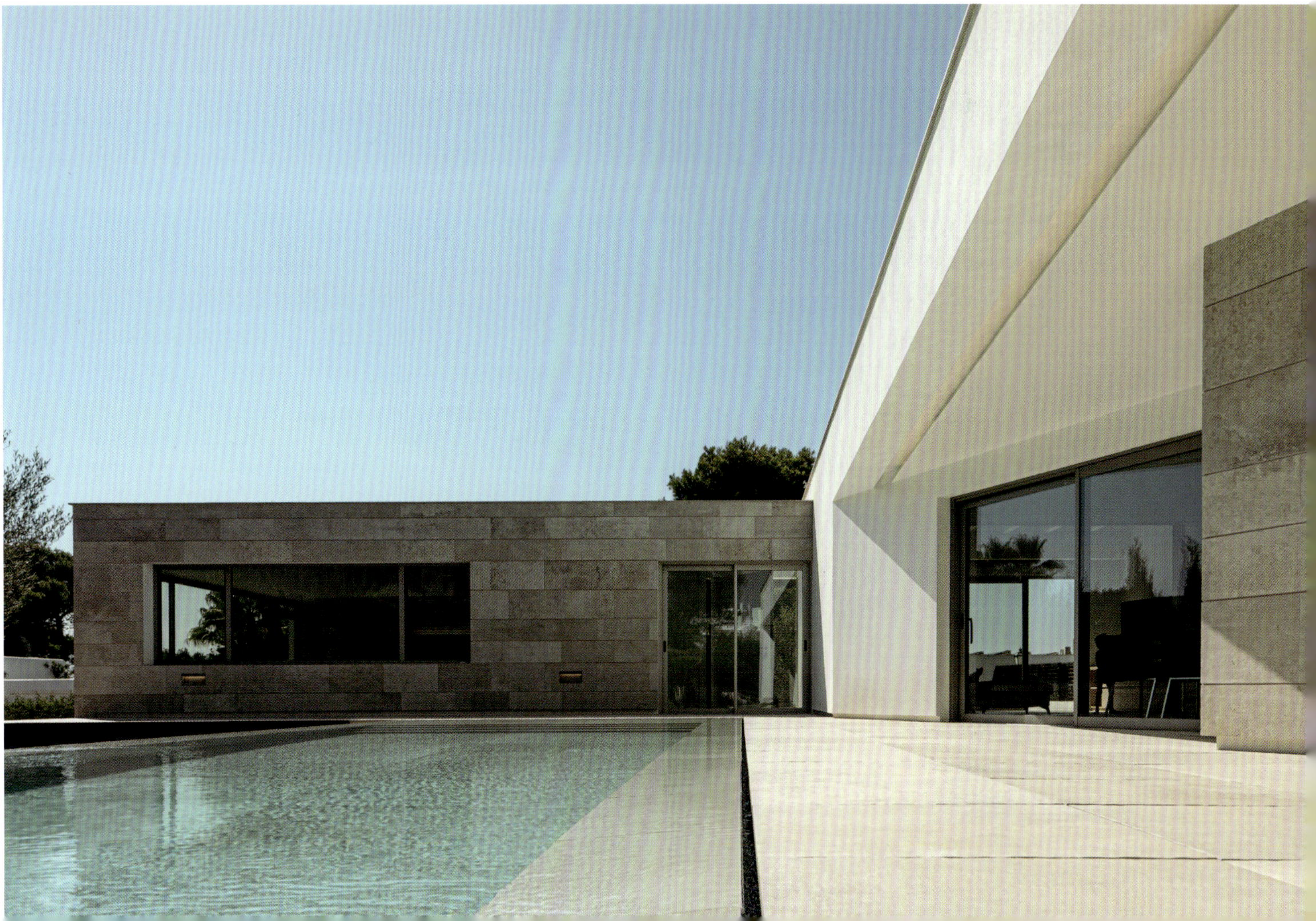

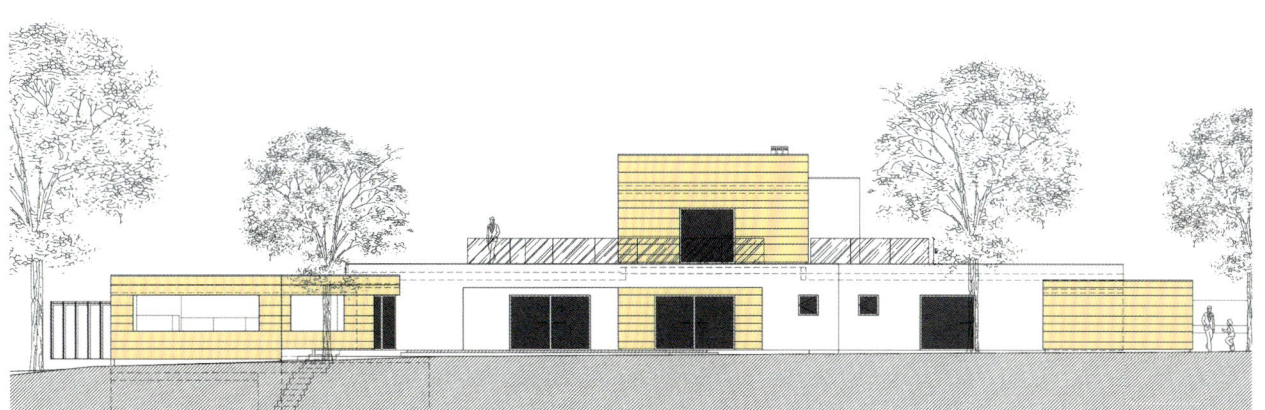

Elevation

ICAZAR ARCHITECTS

PUENTE MILVIO

FELANITX

Photos © Cesc Noguera Fotografía/
Tomeu Canyellas Photography

PALMA CITY

PALMA DE MALLORCA

Photos © Javier de Paz García/estudioballoon

Inspired by Mallorca's rural architecture, this house seeks to "seem as if it has always been there," explain the architects from Icazar. The harmonious integration with the environment, its shape, materials, and stylistic elements make the house a natural part of the landscape.

Situated on a 15,000 m² plot of free and natural space, the location of the construction complies with urban planning regulations, incorporating the existing vegetation and topography in a respectful manner. The winding access road to the house runs among the trees, allowing residents to experience this landscaped microcosm upon arrival at the property.

The project faced the challenge of having to build with modern techniques a work that was meant to look like an old renovated house. For this, materials such as natural stone, micro-cement, cement tiles and wood were used, authentically reflecting the traditional aesthetics of the island. These elements remain in the background and, nevertheless, acquire more character over time.

Inspiriert von der ländlichen Architektur Mallorcas, soll dieses Haus „so aussehen, als ob es schon immer dort gewesen wäre", erklären die Architekten von Icazar. Die harmonische Integration mit der Umgebung, die Form, die Materialien und die stilistischen Elemente machen das Haus zu einem natürlichen Bestandteil der Landschaft.

Auf einem 15.000 m² großen Grundstück aus freiem und natürlichem Raum gelegen, entspricht der Standort des Baus den städtebaulichen Vorschriften und integriert die vorhandene Vegetation und Topographie auf respektvolle Weise. Der gewundene Zufahrtsweg zum Haus führt zwischen den Bäumen hindurch, sodass die Bewohner dieses landschaftlich gestaltete Mikrokosmos bei ihrer Ankunft auf dem Anwesen erleben können.

Das Projekt stellte die Herausforderung dar, mit modernen Techniken ein Werk zu bauen, das wie ein altes renoviertes Haus aussehen sollte. Dafür wurden Materialien wie Naturstein, Mikrozement, Hydraulische Zement Fliesen und Holz verwendet, die authentisch die traditionelle Ästhetik der Insel widerspiegeln. Diese Elemente treten in den Hintergrund und gewinnen dennoch mit der Zeit an Charakter.

Inspirée par l'architecture rurale de Majorque, cette maison cherche à « sembler avoir toujours été là », expliquent les architectes d'Icazar. L'intégration harmonieuse avec l'environnement, sa forme, ses matériaux et ses éléments stylistiques font de la maison une partie naturelle du paysage.

Située sur un terrain de 15 000 m² d'espace libre et naturel, l'emplacement de la construction respecte les réglementations urbanistiques, incorporant de manière respectueuse la végétation et la topographie existantes. Le chemin d'accès sinueux à la maison serpente entre les arbres, permettant aux résidents de découvrir ce microcosme paysager dès leur arrivée sur la propriété.

Le projet a relevé le défi de devoir construire avec des techniques modernes une œuvre censée ressembler à une ancienne maison rénovée. Pour cela, des matériaux tels que la pierre naturelle, le microciment, les carreaux et le bois ont été utilisés, reflétant de manière authentique l'esthétique traditionnelle de l'île. Ces éléments restent en arrière-plan et, néanmoins, acquièrent plus de caractère avec le temps.

Inspirada en la arquitectura rural de Mallorca, esta vivienda busca «parecer haber estado allí desde siempre», explican los arquitectos de Icazar. La integración armoniosa con el entorno de su forma, materiales y elementos estilísticos, convierten la casa en una parte natural del paisaje.

Emplazada en un solar de 15.000 m² de espacio libre y natural, la ubicación de la construcción se ajusta a la normativa urbanística e incorpora de manera respetuosa la vegetación y topografía existentes. El serpenteante camino de acceso a la casa, que discurre entre árboles, permite a los residentes experimentar este microcosmos paisajístico desde su llegada a la propiedad.

El proyecto afrontó el desafío de tener que construir con técnicas modernas una obra que debía tener la apariencia de una antigua casa reformada. Para ello, se emplearon materiales como piedra natural, microcemento, baldosas hidráulicas y madera, que reflejan de forma auténtica la estética tradicional de la isla. Estos elementos permanecen en un segundo plano, y sin embargo adquirirán más carácter con el tiempo.

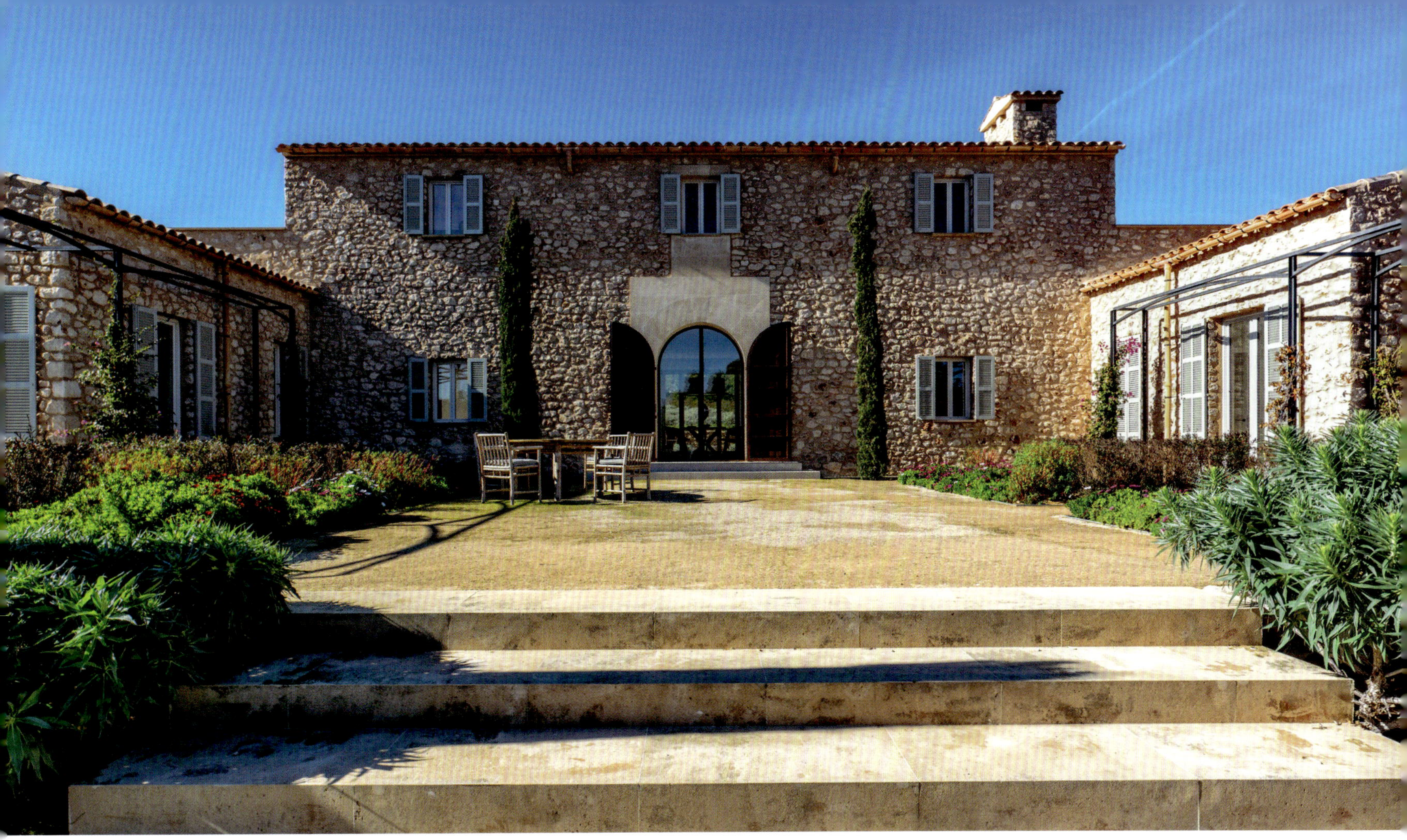

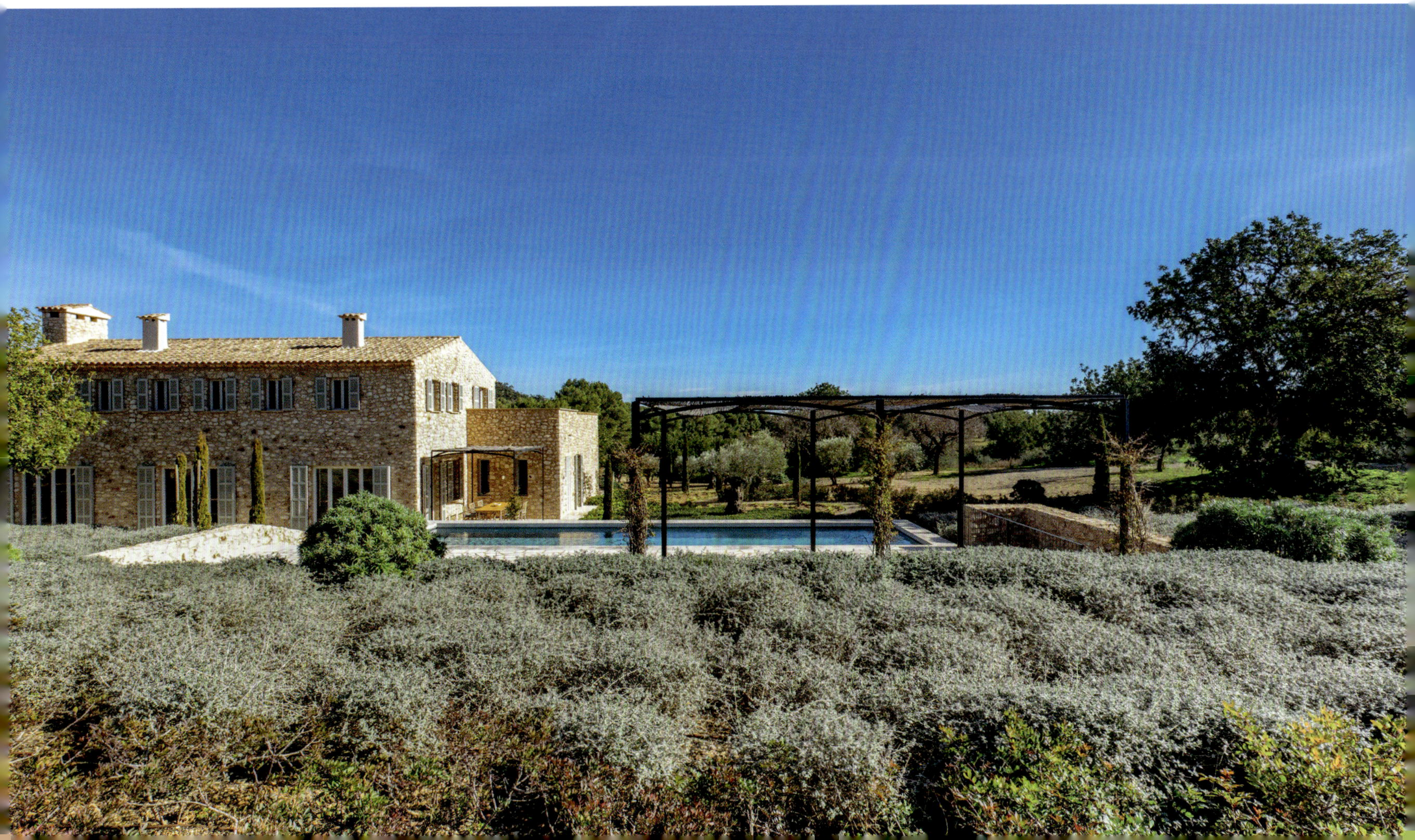

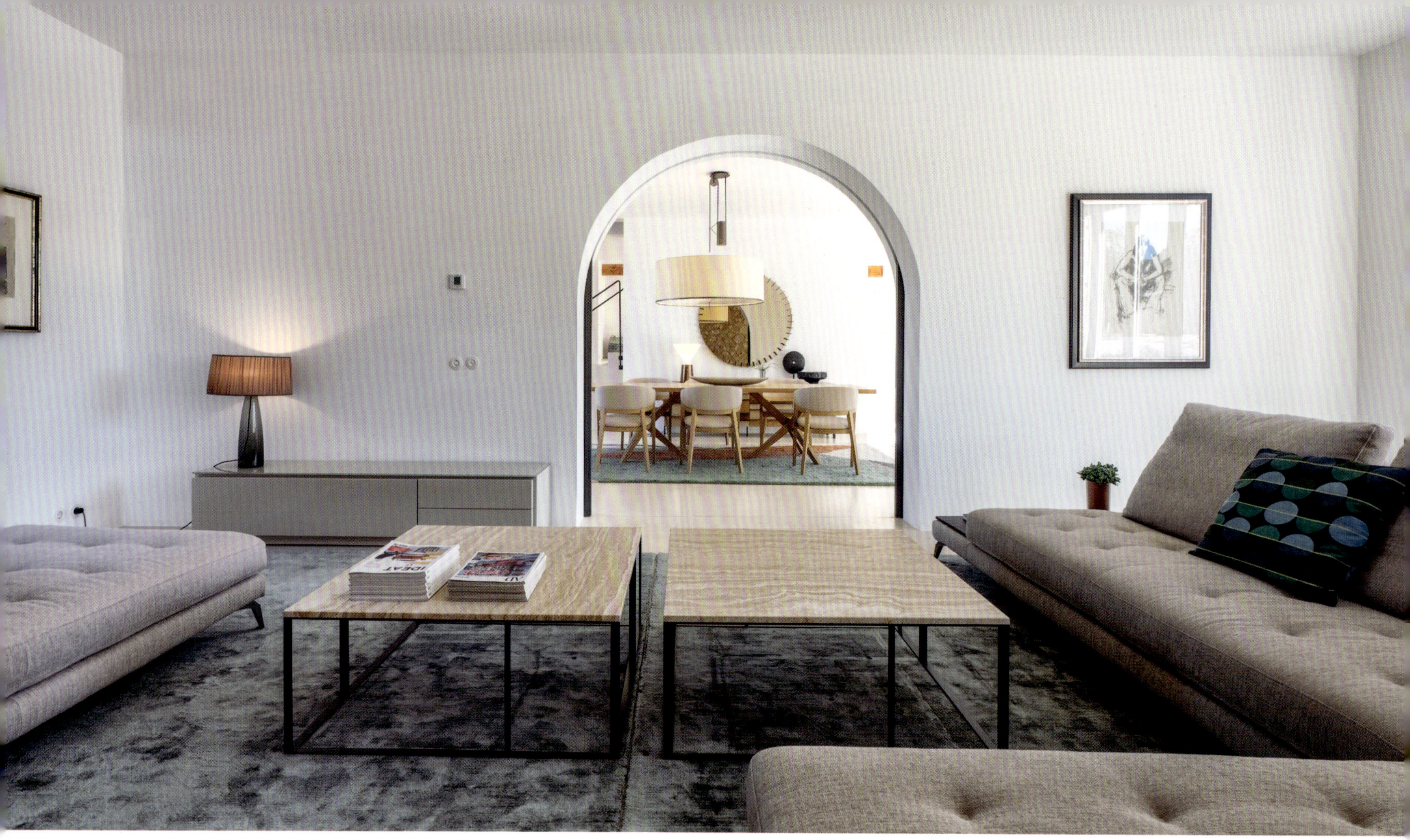

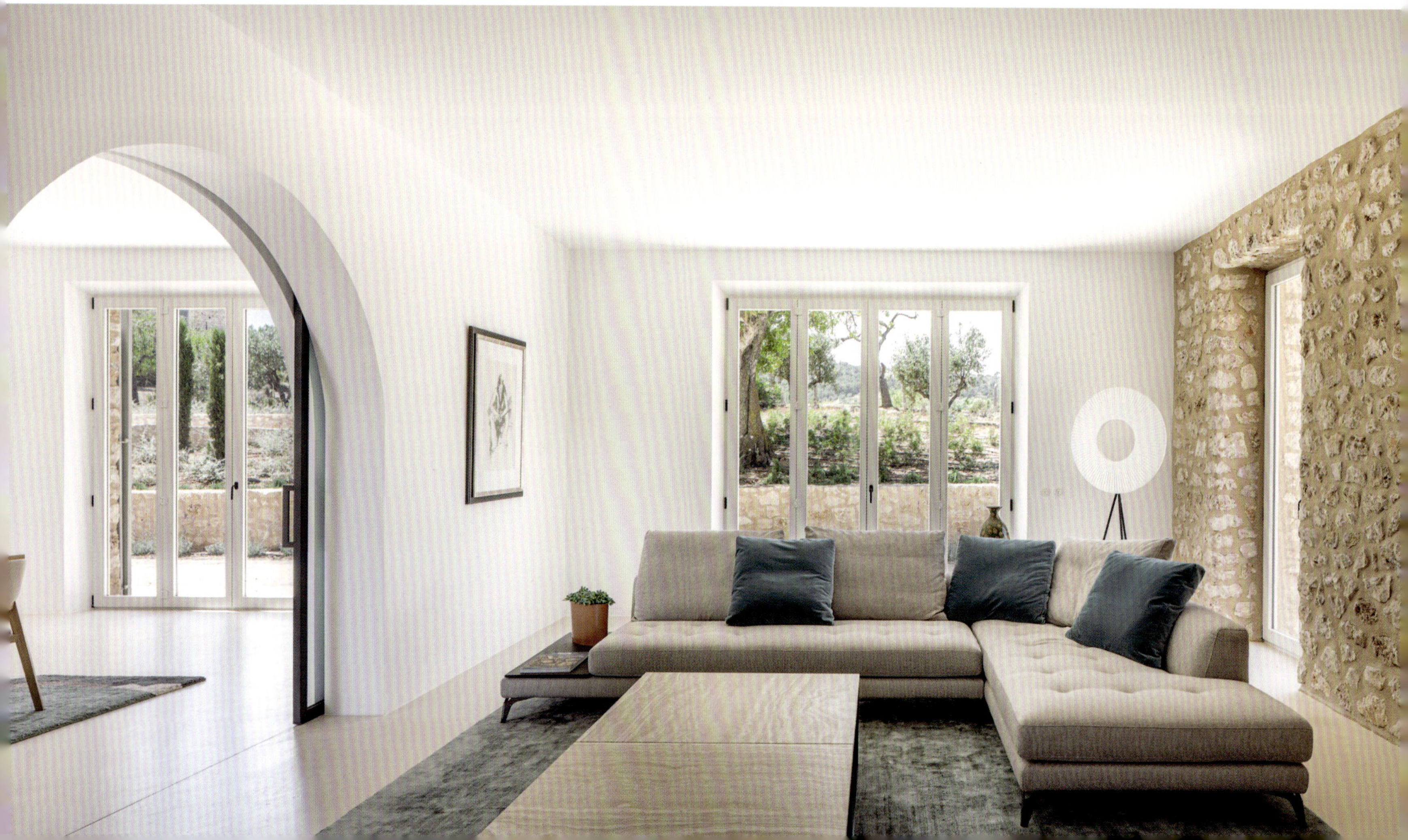

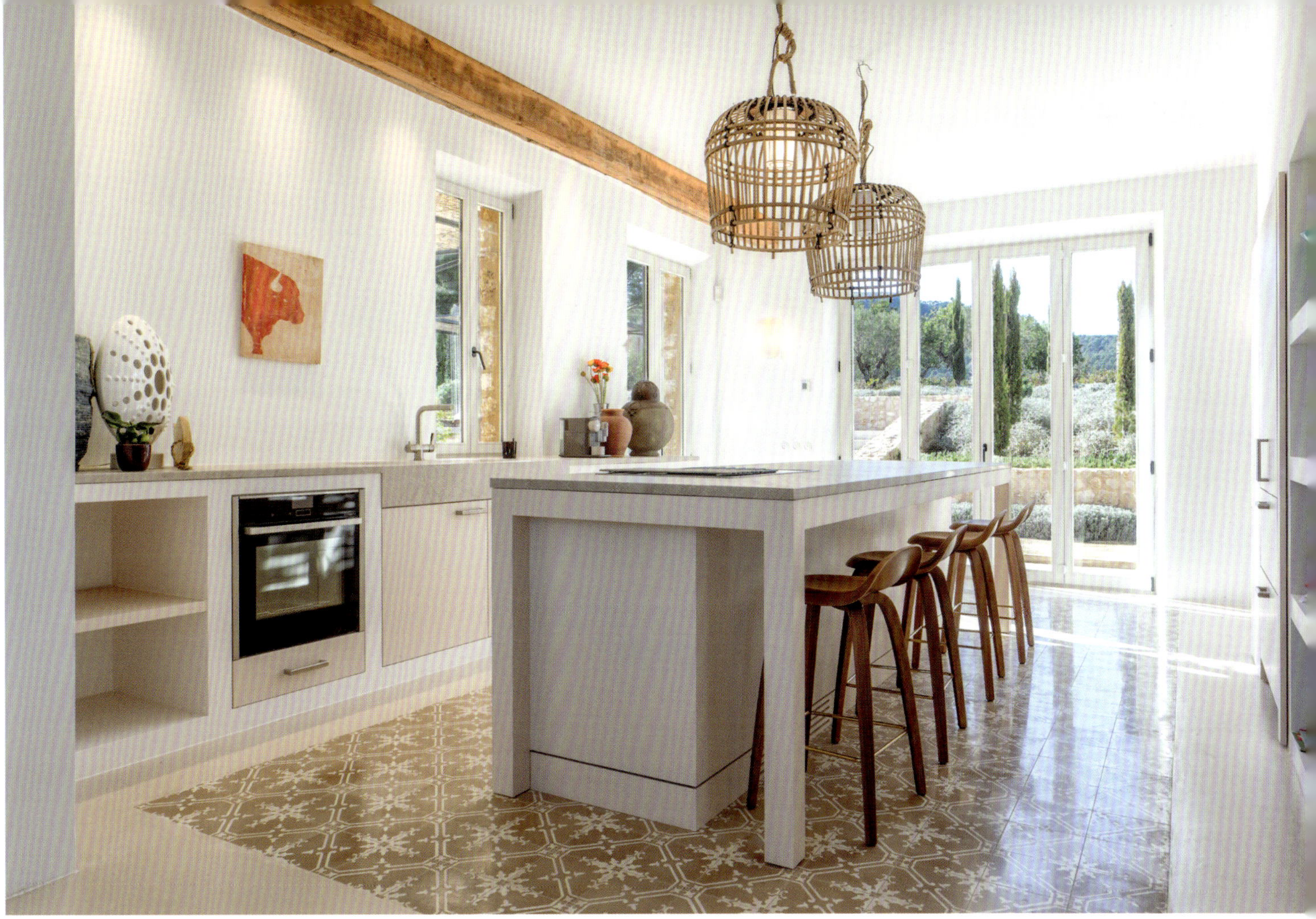

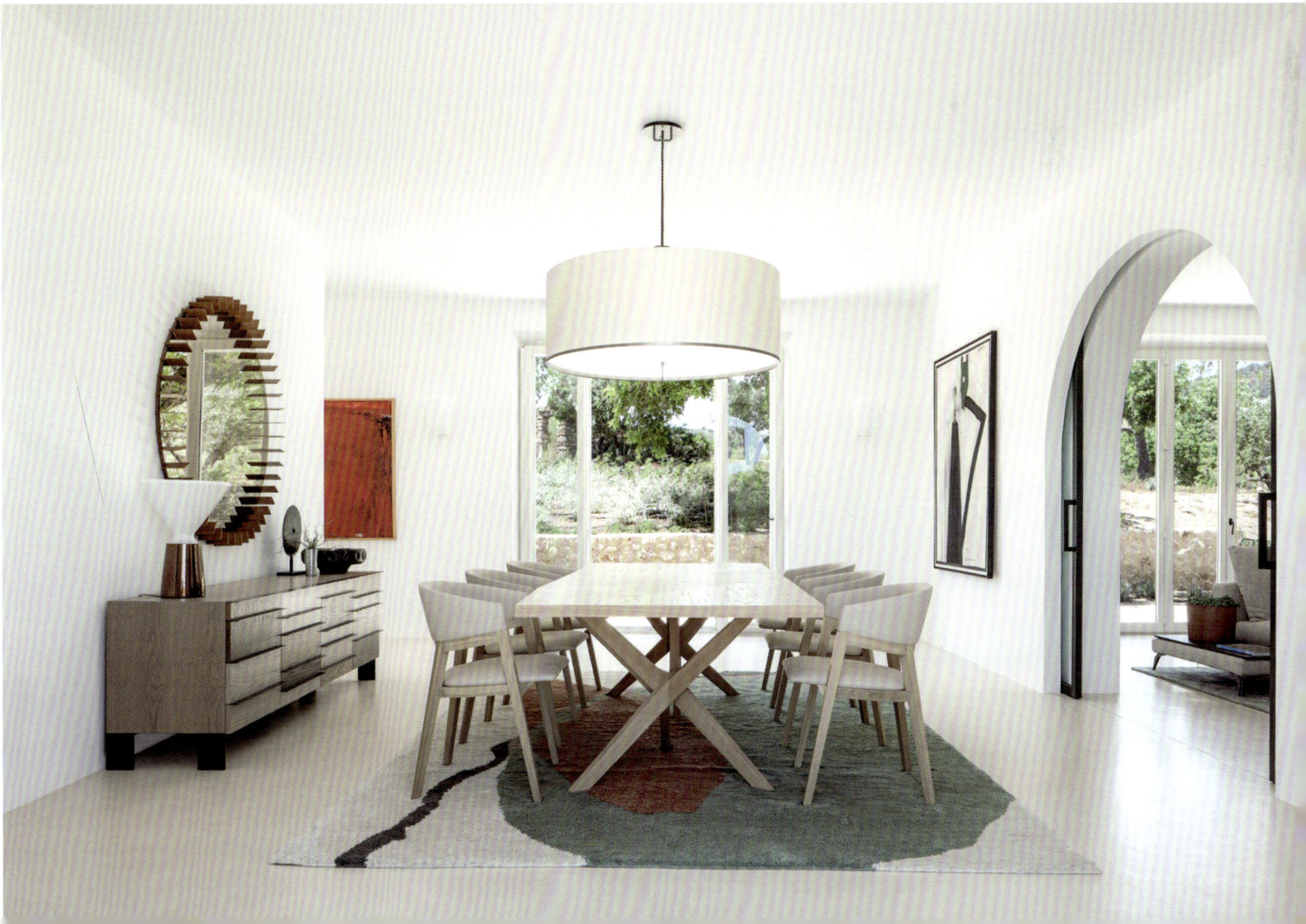

MATERIALS LIKE NATURAL STONE, MICRO-CEMENT,
TILES, AND WOOD WERE USED TO REFLECT THE
ISLAND'S TRADITIONAL AESTHETICS

This house was designed as a minimalist oasis of relaxation in a densely populated urban environment. The project presented the challenge of creating a tranquil space with an interior patio and a pool that contrasts with the cramped feel of the neighborhood. The disorganized neighboring buildings required an architectural calm that was achieved through straight lines and harmonious design. To emphasize this idea, natural and high-quality materials such as light stone on the exterior and dark wood on the interior were used. This reduction to the essentials gives users the opportunity to relax when returning home from bustling urban life. Throughout the different environments of the house, light and shadow, white and black intertwine as a common thread both inside and out. The owner, from the firm Eric Jacobson Design, has been very involved in the design, and most of the furniture has been created by him.
The architectural layout integrates the landscape, generating a variety of outdoor spaces that culminate in the terrace. From there, one can contemplate the bay and the cathedral of Palma with views to lose oneself in at sunset.

Dieses Haus wurde als minimalistisches Entspannungsoase in einer dicht besiedelten urbanen Umgebung entworfen. Das Projekt stellte die Herausforderung dar, einen ruhigen Raum mit einem Innenhof und einem Pool zu schaffen, der im Kontrast zum beengten Gefühl des Viertels steht. Die unorganisierten Nachbargebäude erforderten eine architektonische Ruhe, die durch klare Linien und harmonisches Design erreicht wurde. Um diese Idee zu betonen, wurden natürliche und hochwertige Materialien wie heller Stein außen und dunkles Holz innen verwendet. Diese Reduktion auf das Wesentliche gibt den Nutzern die Möglichkeit, sich zu entspannen, wenn sie aus dem geschäftigen städtischen Leben nach Hause kommen. In den verschiedenen Umgebungen des Hauses verflechten sich Licht und Schatten, Weiß und Schwarz als roter Faden sowohl innen als auch außen. Der Eigentümer, von der Firma Eric Jacobson Design, war sehr in die Gestaltung involviert, und die meisten Möbel wurden von ihm entworfen.
Die architektonische Anordnung integriert die Landschaft und schafft eine Vielzahl von Außenräumen, die in der Terrasse gipfeln. Von dort aus kann man die Bucht und die Kathedrale von Palma mit Blicken genießen, in denen man sich beim Sonnenuntergang verlieren kann.

Cette maison a été conçue comme une oasis minimaliste de détente dans un environnement urbain densément peuplé. Le projet a présenté le défi de créer un espace tranquille avec un patio intérieur et une piscine contrastant avec la sensation d'étroitesse du quartier. Les bâtiments voisins désorganisés nécessitaient une sérénité architecturale, obtenue grâce à des lignes droites et un design harmonieux. Pour souligner cette idée, des matériaux naturels et de haute qualité, comme la pierre claire à l'extérieur et le bois sombre à l'intérieur, ont été utilisés. Cette réduction à l'essentiel offre aux utilisateurs l'occasion de se détendre en rentrant chez eux après une vie urbaine trépidante. Tout au long des différents environnements de la maison, la lumière et l'ombre, le blanc et le noir s'entrelacent comme un fil conducteur à l'intérieur comme à l'extérieur. Le propriétaire, de la société Eric Jacobson Design, a été très impliqué dans la conception et la plupart des meubles ont été conçus par lui.
La disposition architecturale intègre le paysage, générant une variété d'espaces extérieurs qui culminent sur la terrasse. De là, on peut contempler la baie et la cathédrale de Palma avec des vues où se perdre au coucher du soleil.

Esta casa se ha diseñado como un oasis minimalista de relajación en un entorno urbano densamente poblado. El proyecto presentó el desafío de crear un ámbito tranquilo, con un patio interior y una piscina, que contrasta con la sensación de estrechez de espacio del vecindario. Los desestructurados edificios vecinos requerían apostar por una calma arquitectónica, que se logró a través de líneas rectas y un diseño armonioso. Para subrayar esta idea, se utilizaron materiales naturales y de alta calidad, como piedra clara en el exterior y madera oscura en el interior. Esta reducción a lo esencial brinda a los usuarios la oportunidad de relajarse al regresar a casa desde la bulliciosa vida urbana. A lo largo de los diferentes ambientes de la casa, la luz y la sombra, el blanco y el negro, se entrelazan como un hilo conductor, tanto en el interior como en el exterior. El propietario, de la firma Eric Jacobson design, ha estado muy involucrado en el diseño y la mayoría de los muebles han sido creados por él.
La disposición arquitectónica integra el paisaje generando una variedad de espacios al aire libre que culminan en la terraza. Desde allí se contempla la bahía y la catedral de Palma, con unas vistas en las que perderse a la hora del atardecer.

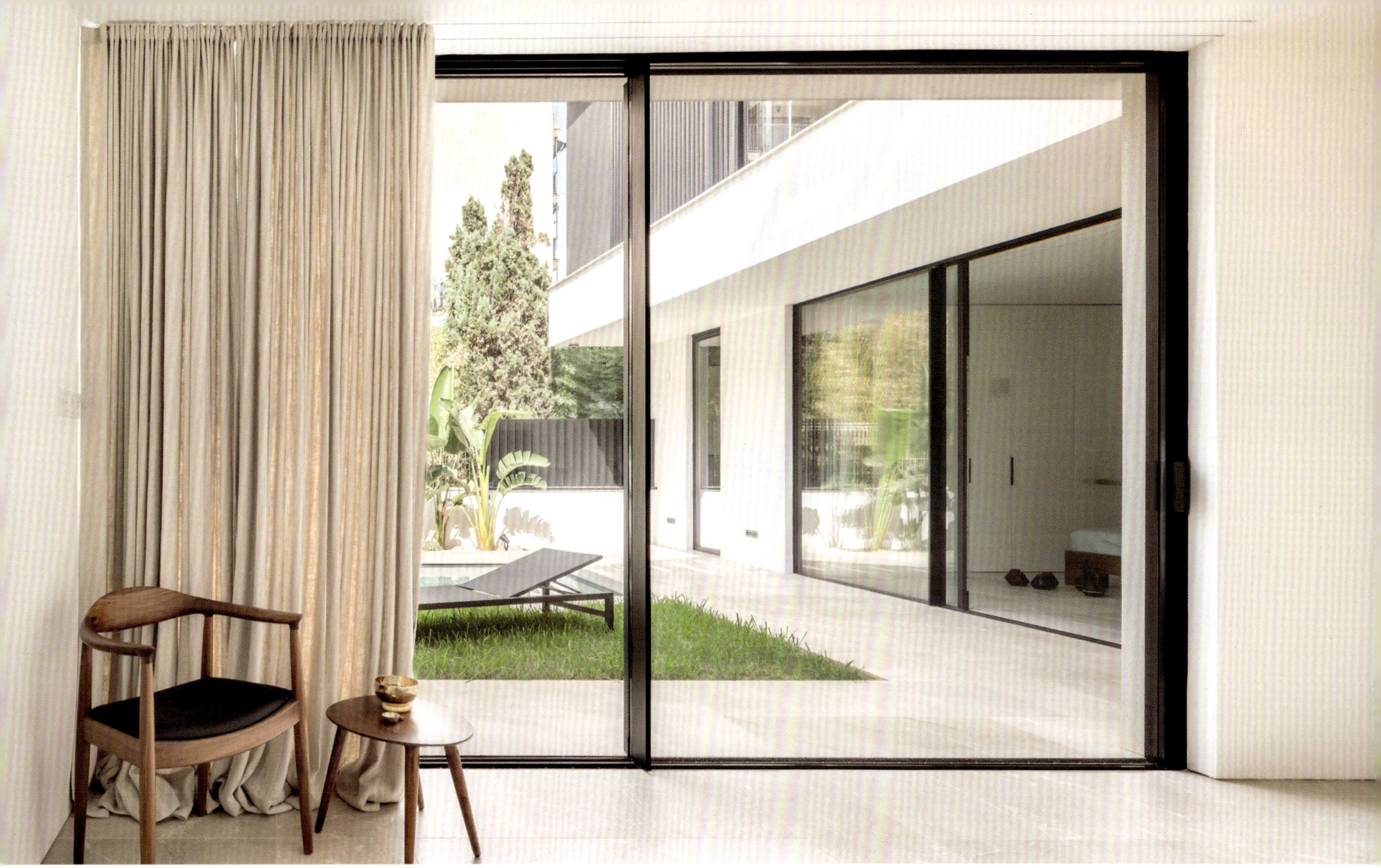

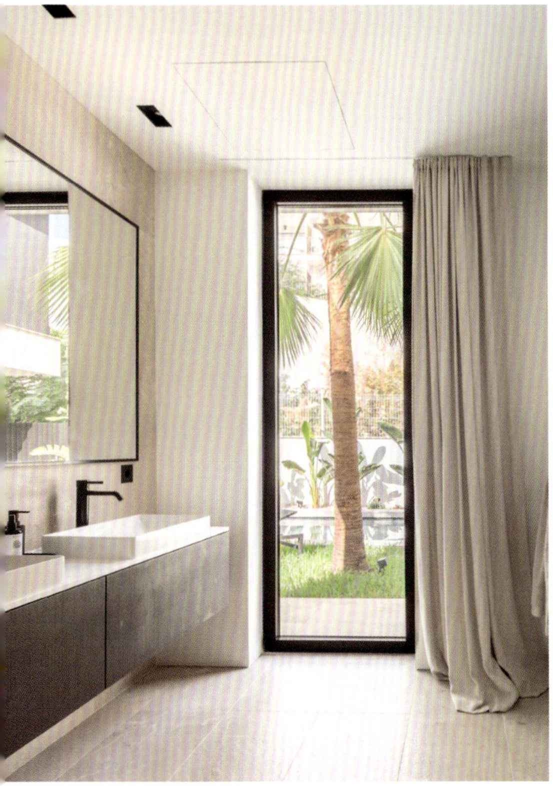

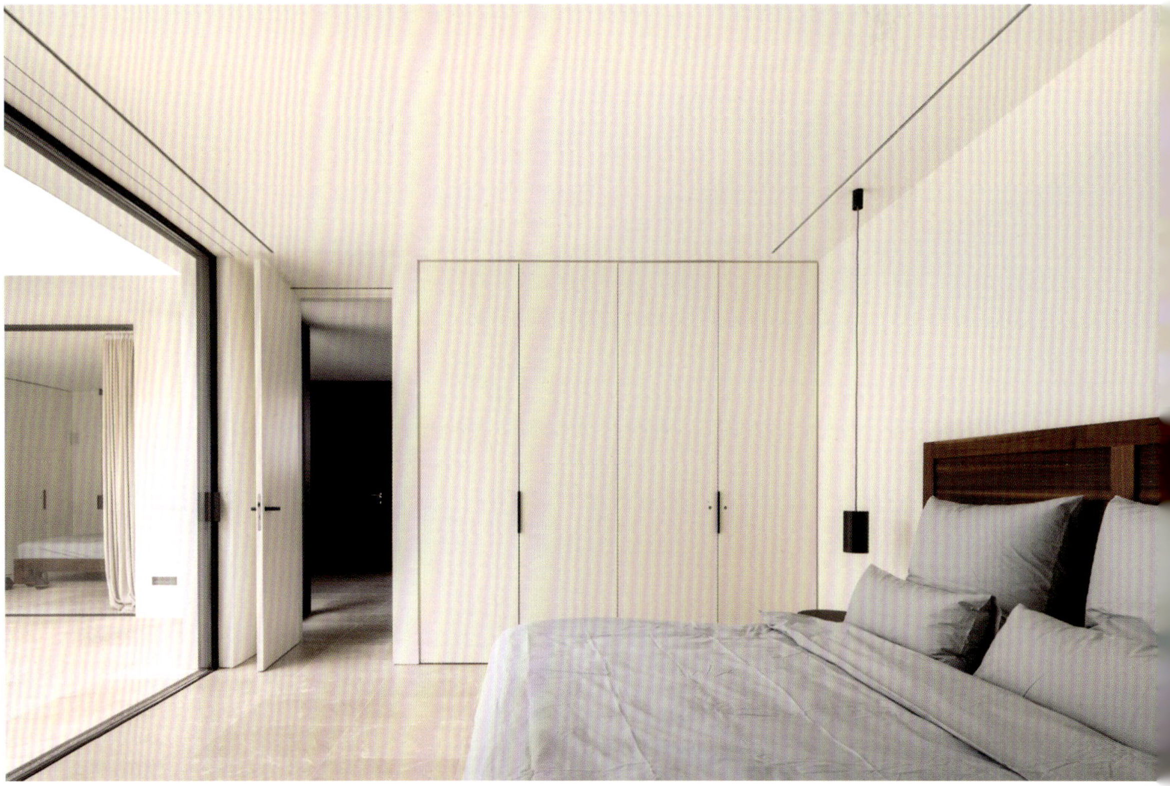

LDFL STUDIO

CASA MARIPOSA

ES CAPDELLÀ

This house is situated on a hilltop surrounded by a privileged environment, part of a protected natural area. However, far from opening up to the surrounding landscape, the interior spaces are characterized by intimacy thanks to a renovation that has remained true to the essence of the existing house.

In addition to a new layout that allowed better use of light and space, the project respected the original spirit of the house while adapting it to contemporary needs without losing its identity. The double-height area, where the kitchen and dining room are located, prioritizes family gatherings around the table.

Original elements such as the tiled roofs and beams were preserved to enhance their classic charm. The interior follows a contemporary rustic Mediterranean style with neutral tones and natural materials that reflect the essence of the island. The lighting enhances each environment, and the new wooden carpentry improved both aesthetics and insulation. The result is a house that blends Mallorcan tradition with contemporary comfort and elegance.

Dieses Haus befindet sich auf einem Hügel, umgeben von einer privilegierten Umgebung, die Teil eines geschützten Naturgebiets ist. Anstatt sich auf die umgebende Landschaft zu öffnen, zeichnen sich die Innenräume durch ihre Intimität aus, dank einer Renovierung, die der Essenz des bestehenden Hauses treu geblieben ist.

Neben einer neuen Aufteilung, die eine bessere Nutzung von Licht und Raum ermöglichte, respektierte das Projekt den ursprünglichen Geist des Hauses und passte es gleichzeitig an zeitgenössische Bedürfnisse an, ohne seine Identität zu verlieren. Der doppelhohe Bereich, in dem sich die Küche und das Esszimmer befinden, legt den Schwerpunkt auf Familientreffen um den Tisch.

Originalelemente wie die Ziegeldächer und Balken wurden erhalten, um ihren klassischen Charme zu betonen. Das Innere folgt einem zeitgenössischen rustikalen mediterranen Stil mit neutralen Tönen und natürlichen Materialien, die das Wesen der Insel widerspiegeln. Die Beleuchtung hebt jede Umgebung hervor, und die neuen Holzarbeiten verbesserten sowohl die Ästhetik als auch die Isolierung. Das Ergebnis ist ein Haus, das die mallorquinische Tradition mit modernem Komfort und Eleganz verbindet.

Cette maison est située sur une colline entourée d'un environnement privilégié, faisant partie d'une zone naturelle protégée. Cependant, loin de s'ouvrir sur le paysage environnant, les espaces intérieurs se caractérisent par leur intimité grâce à une rénovation qui est restée fidèle à l'essence de la maison existante.

En plus d'une nouvelle disposition qui permettait une meilleure utilisation de la lumière et de l'espace, le projet a respecté l'esprit original de la maison tout en l'adaptant aux besoins contemporains sans perdre son identité. La zone à double hauteur, où se trouvent la cuisine et la salle à manger, privilégie les rassemblements familiaux autour de la table.

Des éléments originaux tels que les toits en tuiles et les poutres ont été conservés pour rehausser leur charme classique. L'intérieur suit un style rustique méditerranéen contemporain avec des tons neutres et des matériaux naturels qui reflètent l'essence de l'île. L'éclairage met en valeur chaque environnement et les nouvelles menuiseries en bois ont amélioré à la fois l'esthétique et l'isolation. Le résultat est une maison qui fusionne la tradition majorquine avec le confort et l'élégance contemporains.

Esta vivienda se sitúa en lo alto de una colina rodeada de un entorno privilegiado parte de un espacio natural protegido. Sin embargo, lejos de abrirse al paisaje circundante, los espacios interiores se caracterizan por la intimidad gracias a una reforma que ha sido fiel a la esencia de la vivienda existente.

Aparte de una nueva distribución que permitió aprovechar mejor la luz y la escala de los espacios, el proyecto respetó el espíritu original de la casa adaptándola a las necesidades contemporáneas sin perder su identidad. Destaca el área de doble altura donde se decidió colocar la cocina y el comedor y privilegiar los momentos de reunión familiar alrededor de la mesa.

Se mantuvieron elementos originales como las cubiertas de teja y las vigas, para potenciar su encanto clásico. En el interior, se siguió un estilo contemporáneo rústico mediterráneo, con tonos neutros y materiales naturales que reflejan la esencia de la isla. La iluminación realza cada ambiente y las nuevas carpinterías de madera mejoraron tanto la estética como el aislamiento. El resultado es una casa que fusiona la tradición mallorquina con el confort y la elegancia contemporánea.

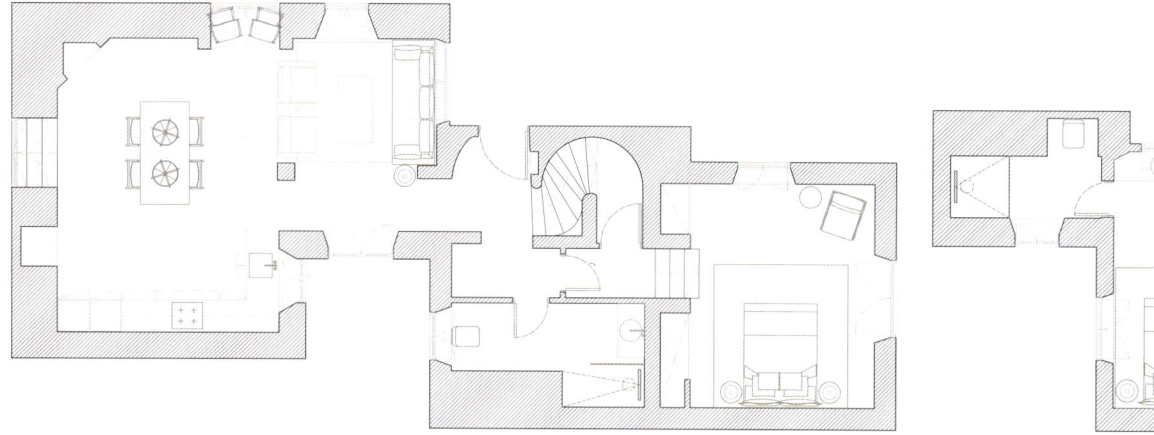

Ground floor plan

First floor plan

THE RENOVATION HAS REMAINED TRUE TO THE
ESSENCE OF THE EXISTING HOUSE

LERYCKEMARTI
DESIGN

CAN SERRA

SERRA DE TRAMUNTANA, POLLENÇA

Photos © Antoni Perello Valls

Eclectic fusion is the hallmark of this new construction. Here, the contemporary intermingles with the traditional, giving life to a space where exposed concrete ceilings and technical lighting dialogue with the heritage of sloped ceilings, beams, railings, and banisters. The batiporte —a typical Mallorcan door type— and a pebble floor are elements rooted in the rich tradition of Balearic mountain architecture that complete this property.

The decoration features large-scale furniture and pieces such as a spacious cupboard and a long dining table. A medieval tapestry adorning the foyer wall stands out. The interior designers incorporated details of classic Mallorcan decoration, such as wardrobe doors with motifs reminiscent of carriage houses, stair railings, and paneled doors. In the kitchen, industrial stainless steel contrasts with the Mallorcan stone sink and an old wooden dining table. The fireplace installed on a concrete base integrates the ceilings and creates a cozy living room in line with the mountain houses of the Tramuntana mountains.

Eklektische Fusion ist das Markenzeichen dieses Neubaus. Hier vermischt sich das Zeitgenössische mit dem Traditionellen und belebt einen Raum, in dem freiliegende Betondecken und technische Beleuchtung mit dem Erbe von Schrägdächern, Balken, Balustraden und Geländern im Dialog stehen. Das batiporte - eine typische mallorquinische Tür - und ein Kiesboden sind Elemente, die in der reichen Tradition der balearischen Bergarchitektur verwurzelt sind und diese Immobilie vervollständigen.

Die Dekoration verwendet große Möbelstücke und Elemente wie einen geräumigen Schrank und einen langen Esstisch. Eine mittelalterliche Tapisserie schmückt die Wand des Foyers. Die Innendesigner haben Details der klassischen mallorquinischen Dekoration integriert, wie Schranktüren mit Motiven, die an Kutschenhäuser erinnern, Treppengeländer und getäfelte Türen. In der Küche kontrastiert der industriell anmutende Edelstahl mit dem mallorquinischen Steinausschnitt und einem alten Holztisch. Der auf einer Betonbasis installierte Kamin integriert die Decken und schafft ein gemütliches Wohnzimmer im Einklang mit den Berghäusern der Serra de Tramuntana.

La fusion éclectique est la marque distinctive de cette nouvelle construction. Ici, le contemporain s'entrelace avec le traditionnel, donnant vie à un espace où les plafonds en béton apparent et l'éclairage technique dialoguent avec l'héritage des plafonds inclinés, des poutres, des balustrades et des rampes. Le batiporte – un type de porte typique de Majorque – et un sol en galets sont des éléments enracinés dans la riche tradition de l'architecture de montagne baléare qui complètent cette propriété.

La décoration recourt à des meubles et pièces de grandes dimensions comme une vaste armoire et une longue table à manger. Une tapisserie médiévale orne le mur du hall d'entrée. Les designers d'intérieur ont intégré des détails de la décoration classique majorquine, tels que les portes d'armoire avec des motifs rappelant les remises de voitures, les rampes d'escalier et les portes à panneaux. Dans la cuisine, l'acier inoxydable de caractère industriel contraste avec l'évier en pierre majorquine et une table à manger en bois ancien. La cheminée installée sur une base en béton intègre les plafonds et crée un salon accueillant en ligne avec les maisons de montagne de la Serra de Tramuntana.

La fusión ecléctica es el sello distintivo de esta obra nueva. Aquí, lo contemporáneo se entrelaza con lo tradicional, dando vida a un espacio donde los techos de hormigón visto y la iluminación técnica dialogan con la herencia de techos inclinados, vigas, barandillas y pasamanos. El batiporte —un tipo de puerta típica de Mallorca— y el suelo de canto rodado, son elementos arraigados en la rica tradición de la arquitectura de montaña balear que completan esta propiedad.

La decoración recurre a mobiliario y piezas de grandes dimensiones, como una amplia alacena y una larga mesa de comedor. Destaca el tapiz medieval que adorna la pared del recibidor. Los interioristas incorporaron detalles de la decoración clásica mallorquina, como las puertas de armario con motivos que recuerdan las cocheras, los pasamanos en la escalera principal y las puertas plafonadas. En la cocina, el acero inoxidable de marcado carácter industrial, contrasta con la pica de piedra y una mesa de comedor de madera antigua. La chimenea, instalada sobre una base de hormigón, integra los techos y crea un salón acogedor, en línea con las casas de montaña de la Serra de Tramuntana.

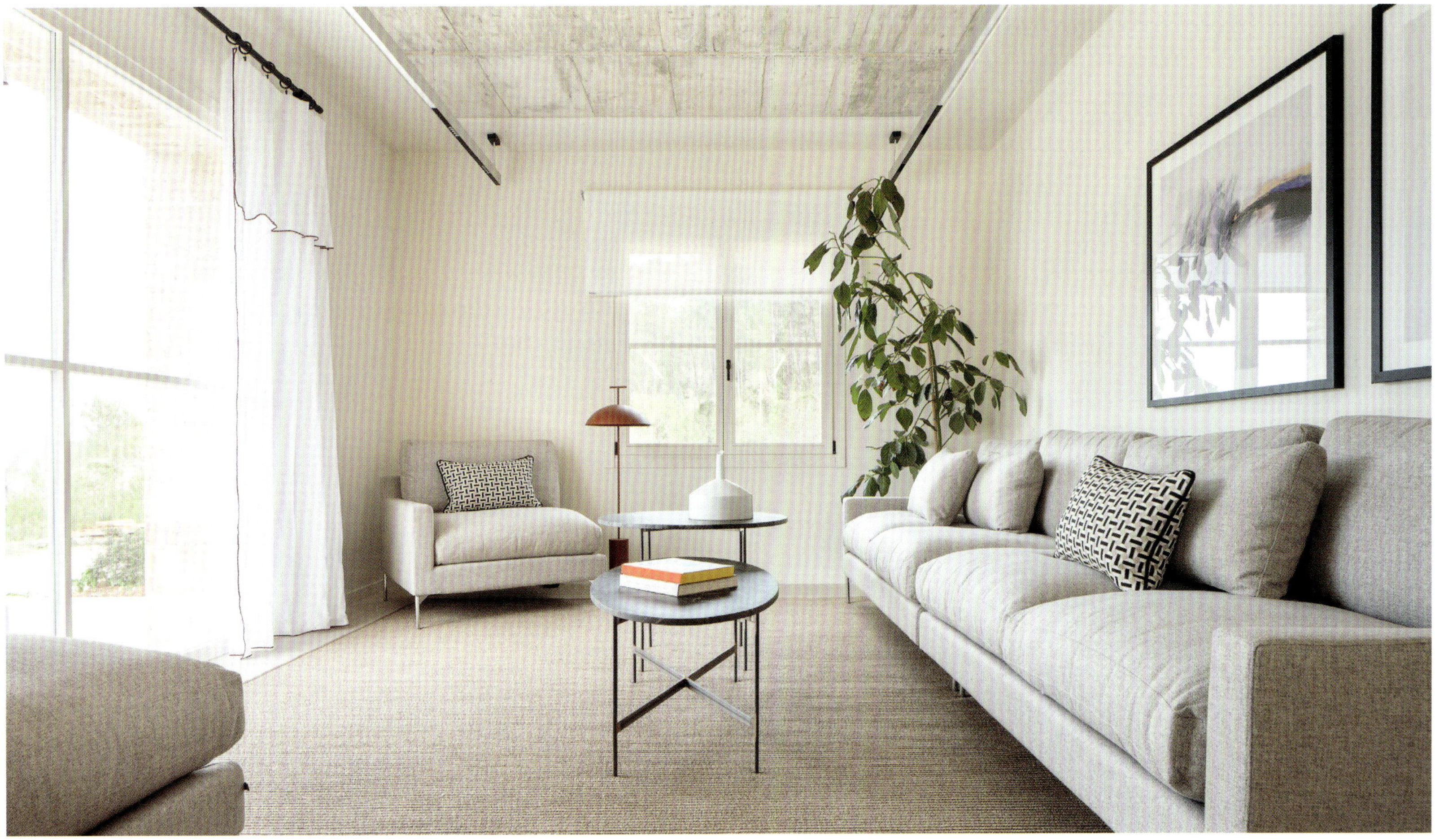

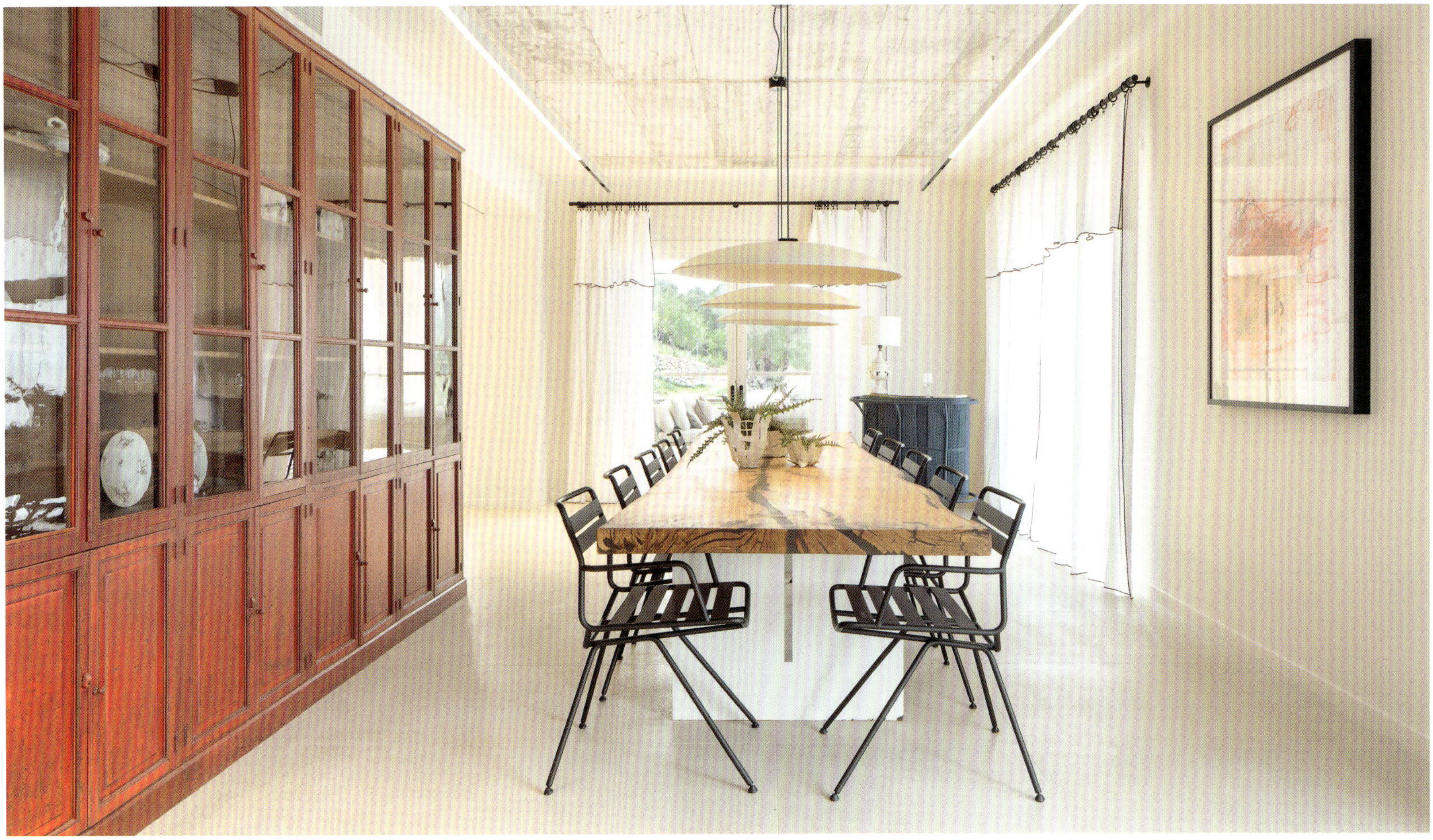

THE CONTEMPORARY INTERMINGLES WITH THE TRADITIONAL
IN THIS HOUSE IN SERRA DE TRAMUNTANA

LF91 DESIGN
CONSULTANTS

CAN PATRÓ

POLLENÇA

The result of the renovation of two emblematic buildings with a palatial air in the historic center of Pollença, Can Patró houses timeless homes with a shared central courtyard that evokes the calm of the Mediterranean. The transformation, led by LF91 and its interior designer Marta Jáudenes, together with architect Jaume Alomar from Missio 21, has recovered existing tiles in pavements and vertical parameters and traditional materials such as Mallorcan Marés stone.

The larger building is located on Calle Mayor, and its façade was meticulously restored to preserve all decorative components and original finishes. It is a three-story building with galleries and pillars, where the balconies of the shop it housed on the first floor have been maintained. The courtyard between both renovated buildings is an oasis of calm with a pool that provides natural light and ventilation to all rooms. The high-quality materials and carpentry restorations have achieved a perfect balance between historical preservation and modern functionality.

Das Ergebnis der Renovierung von zwei emblematischen Gebäuden mit palatialem Flair im historischen Zentrum von Pollença, Can Patró beherbergt zeitlose Häuser mit einem gemeinsamen Innenhof, der die Ruhe des Mittelmeers widerspiegelt. Bei der Umgestaltung, die von LF91 und seiner Innenarchitektin Marta Jáudenes zusammen mit dem Architekten Jaume Alomar von Missio 21 durchgeführt wurde, wurden vorhandene Fliesen in den Gehwegen und vertikalen Parametern sowie traditionelle Materialien wie der mallorquinische Marés-Stein wiederverwendet.

Das größere Gebäude befindet sich in der Calle Mayor, und seine Fassade wurde sorgfältig restauriert, um alle dekorativen Komponenten und ursprünglichen Oberflächen zu bewahren. Es handelt sich um ein dreistöckiges Gebäude mit Galerien und Säulen, bei dem die Balkone des im ersten Stock untergebrachten Geschäfts erhalten wurden. Der Innenhof zwischen den beiden renovierten Gebäuden ist eine Oase der Ruhe mit einem Pool, der allen Räumen natürliches Licht und Belüftung bietet. Hochwertige Materialien und Tischlerarbeiten haben ein perfektes Gleichgewicht zwischen historischer Erhaltung und moderner Funktionalität erreicht.

Le résultat de la rénovation de deux bâtiments emblématiques à l'air palatial dans le centre historique de Pollença, Can Patró abrite des maisons intemporelles avec une cour centrale partagée qui évoque le calme de la Méditerranée. La transformation, dirigée par LF91 et son architecte d'intérieur Marta Jáudenes, en collaboration avec l'architecte Jaume Alomar de Missio 21, a récupéré des carreaux existants dans les pavements et paramètres verticaux et des matériaux traditionnels comme la pierre marés majorquine.

Le bâtiment le plus volumineux est situé sur la Calle Mayor, et sa façade a été méticuleusement restaurée pour préserver tous les composants décoratifs et finitions originales. Il s'agit d'une construction de trois étages avec des galeries et des piliers, où les balcons du commerce qu'il abritait au premier étage ont été maintenus. La cour entre les deux bâtiments rénovés est un oasis de calme avec une piscine qui apporte lumière naturelle et ventilation à toutes les pièces. Les matériaux de qualité et les restaurations de menuiserie ont réussi à atteindre un équilibre parfait entre la préservation historique et la fonctionnalité moderne.

Resultado de la reforma de dos edificios emblemáticos con aire palaciego en el centro histórico de Pollença, Can Patró aloja unas viviendas de aire atemporal con un patio central compartido que evoca la calma del Mediterráneo. La transformación que estuvo a cargo de LF91 y su interiorista Marta Jáudenes, junto al arquitecto Jaume Alomar de Missio 21, ha recuperado baldosas existentes en pavimentos y parámetros verticales, y materiales tradicionales como la piedra mallorquina Marés.

El edificio más voluminoso está situado en la Calle Mayor y su fachada se restauró muy meticulosamente para preservar todos los componentes decorativos y acabados originales. Se trata de una edificación de tres plantas con galerías y pilares en la que se han mantenido los balcones del comercio que alojaba en la primera planta. El patio entre ambas edificaciones reformadas es un oasis de calma con piscina que proporciona luz natural y ventilación a todas las estancias. Los materiales de calidad y las restauraciones de carpinterías han logrado un perfecto equilibrio entre la preservación histórica y la funcionalidad moderna.

Façade

HIGH-QUALITY MATERIALS AND CARPENTRY HAVE BALANCED
HISTORICAL PRESERVATION WITH MODERN FUNCTIONALITY

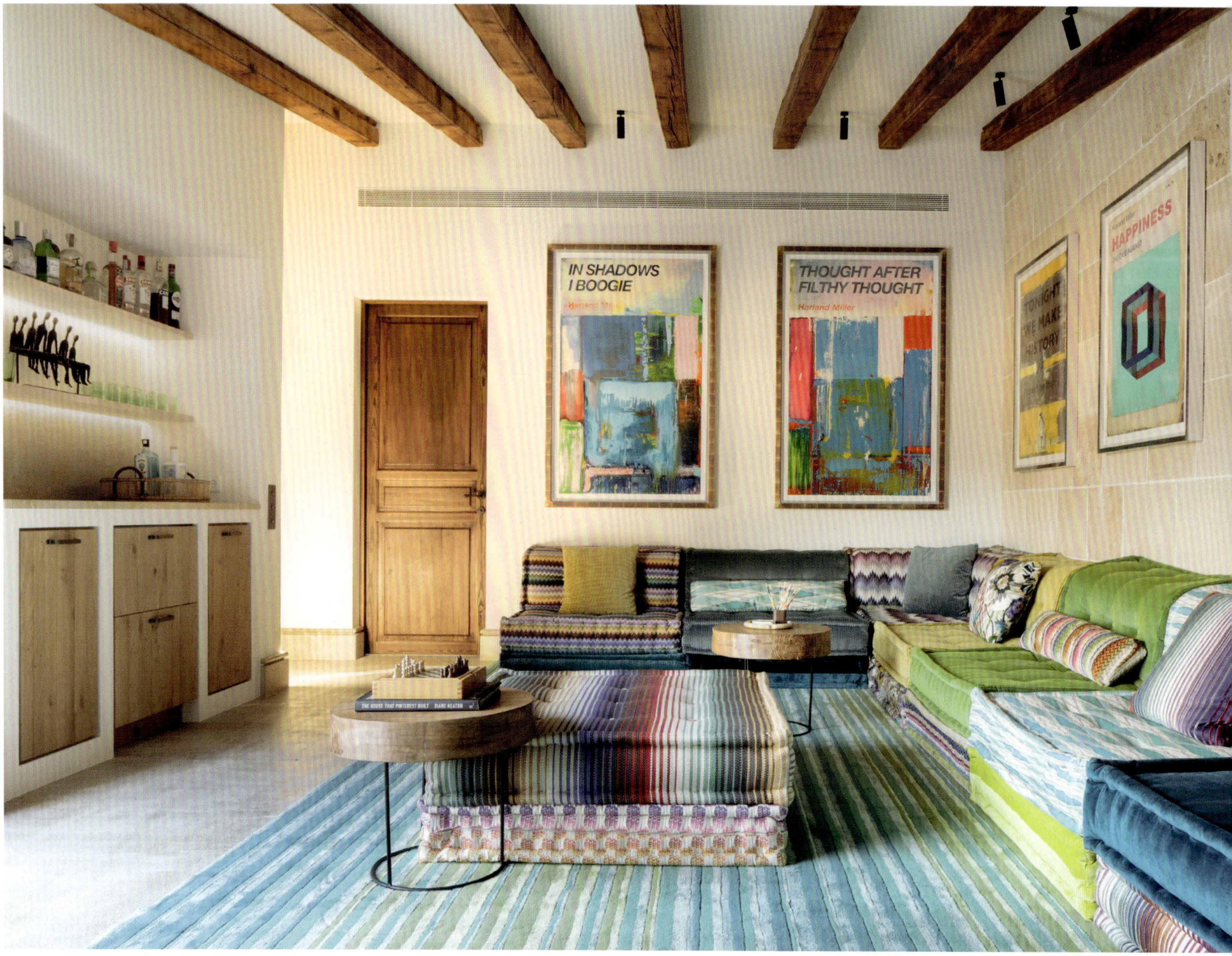
IN SHADOWS
I BOOGIE
THOUGHT AFTER
FILTHY THOUGHT
Harland Miller
HAPPINESS
TONIGHT
WE MAKE
HISTORY

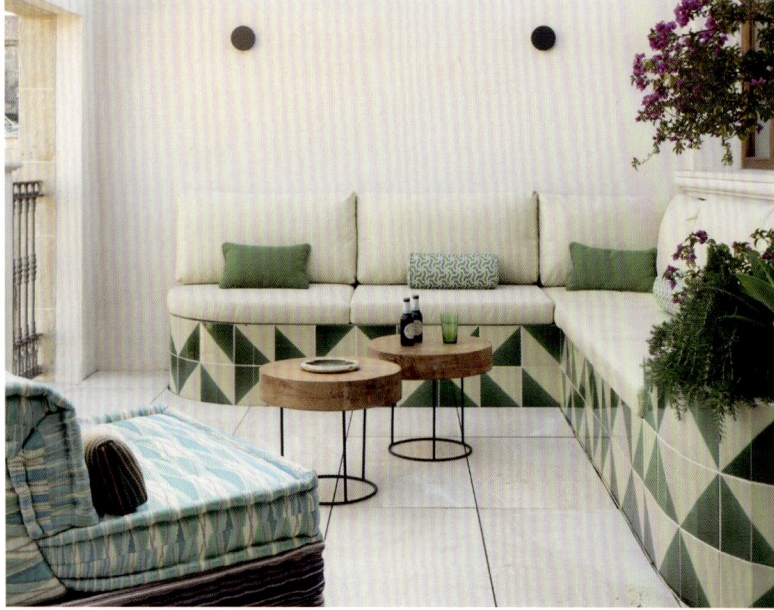

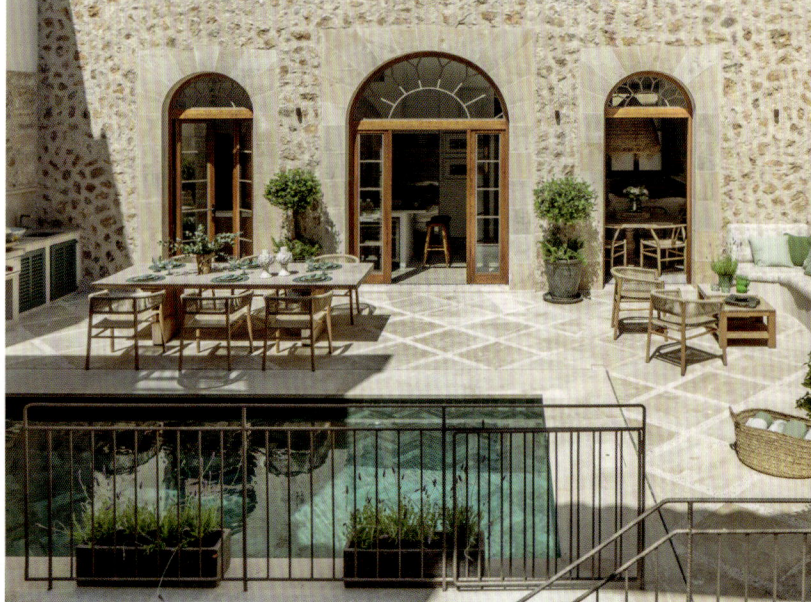

MARIA RAMIS ARCHITECTURE

CASA H

MOSCARI

Photos © Tomeu Canyelles

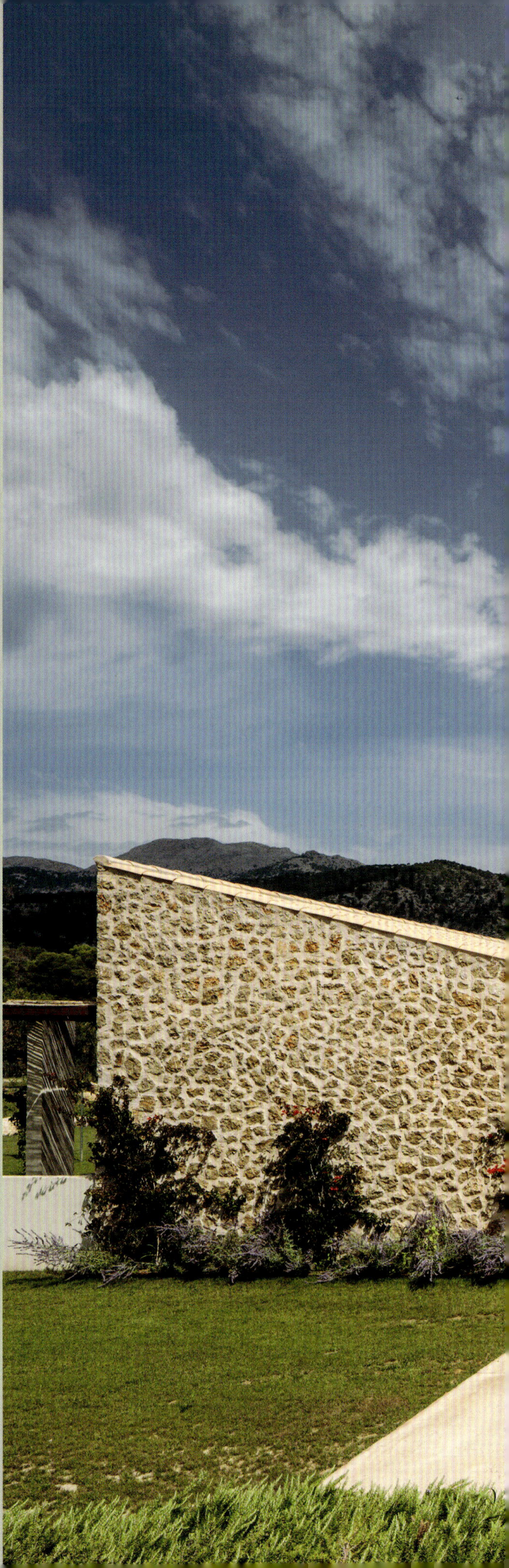

In the idyllic village of Moscari, with just 400 inhabitants, this estate embraces the magnificent views of the Serra de Tramuntana and the bay of Alcudia. The house unfolds on a single floor, integrating with the landscape. The construction has a distinctive H-shape, creating two large open courtyards. These courtyards divide the two main volumes of the house: the daytime area and the nighttime area. Both spaces are separated by the entrance area to the house.

The architect, Maria Ramis, an advocate for simplicity and brightness, designed the house so that natural light and views of the landscape flow inside without interruption. Traditional materials such as natural stone from Binissalem and wood for the beams preserve the local character of the house. The porch beams are made with reeds from the Albufera of Mallorca, while the interior floors feature polished concrete and river stones for the access area. This fusion of elements brings warmth and balance to both the interior and exterior of the house, enhancing the appeal of Mallorcan architecture in every detail.

Im idyllischen Dorf Moscari, mit nur 400 Einwohnern, umfasst dieses Anwesen die herrlichen Ausblicke auf die Serra de Tramuntana und die Bucht von Alcudia. Das Haus erstreckt sich über eine einzige Etage und integriert sich in die Landschaft. Das Haus hat eine charakteristische H-Form, die zwei große offene Höfe schafft. Diese Höfe teilen die beiden Hauptvolumen des Hauses: den Tagesbereich und den Nachtbereich. Beide Räume sind durch den Eingangsbereich des Hauses getrennt.

Der Architekt, Maria Ramis, ein Befürworter von Einfachheit und Helligkeit, gestaltete das Haus so, dass das natürliche Licht und die Aussicht auf die Landschaft ununterbrochen ins Innere fließen. Traditionelle Materialien wie der Naturstein aus Binissalem und Holz für die Balken bewahren den lokalen Charakter des Hauses. Die Balken der Veranden sind aus Schilf vom Albufera von Mallorca gefertigt, während die Innenböden aus poliertem Beton und Flusssteinen für den Zugangsbereich bestehen. Diese Verschmelzung von Elementen bringt Wärme und Ausgewogenheit sowohl ins Innere als auch ins Äußere des Hauses und verstärkt den Reiz der mallorquinischen Architektur in jedem Detail.

Dans le village idyllique de Moscari, avec seulement 400 habitants, cette propriété embrasse les vues magnifiques sur la Serra de Tramuntana et la baie d'Alcudia. La maison se déploie sur un seul étage, s'intégrant au paysage. La construction a une forme distinctive en H, créant deux grandes cours ouvertes. Ces cours divisent les deux volumes principaux de la maison : la zone de jour et la zone de nuit. Les deux espaces sont séparés par l'aire d'entrée de la maison.

L'architecte, Maria Ramis, défenseur de la simplicité et de la luminosité, a conçu la maison pour que la lumière naturelle et les vues sur le paysage pénètrent à l'intérieur sans interruption. Les matériaux traditionnels comme la pierre naturelle de Binissalem et le bois pour les poutres préservent le caractère local de la maison. Les poutres des porches sont faites avec des roseaux de l'Albufera de Majorque, tandis que les sols intérieurs présentent du béton poli et des galets pour la zone d'accès. Cette fusion d'éléments apporte chaleur et équilibre à l'intérieur comme à l'extérieur de la maison, renforçant l'attrait de l'architecture majorquine dans chaque détail.

En el idílico pueblo de Moscari, de apenas 400 habitantes, se erige esta finca que abraza las magníficas vistas de la Serra de Tramuntana y la bahía de Alcudia. La casa se despliega en una sola planta integrándose al paisaje. La vivienda tiene una distintiva forma de H, que genera dos grandes patios abiertos. Estos patios dividen los dos volúmenes principales de la casa: la zona de día y la zona de noche. Ambos espacios están separados por el área de la entrada a la vivienda.

La arquitecta, Maria Ramis, defensora de la sencillez y la luminosidad, diseñó la casa para que la luz natural y las vistas al paisaje fluyan al interior sin interrupciones. Los materiales tradicionales, como la piedra natural de Binissalem y la madera para las viguetas preservan el carácter local de la casa. El entrevigado de los porches está hecho con cañas de la Albufera de Mallorca, mientras que los pavimentos interiores lucen hormigón pulido y piedras de canto rodado para la zona de acceso. Esta fusión de elementos otorga calidez y equilibrio tanto al interior como al exterior de la casa, potenciando el atractivo de la arquitectura mallorquina en cada detalle.

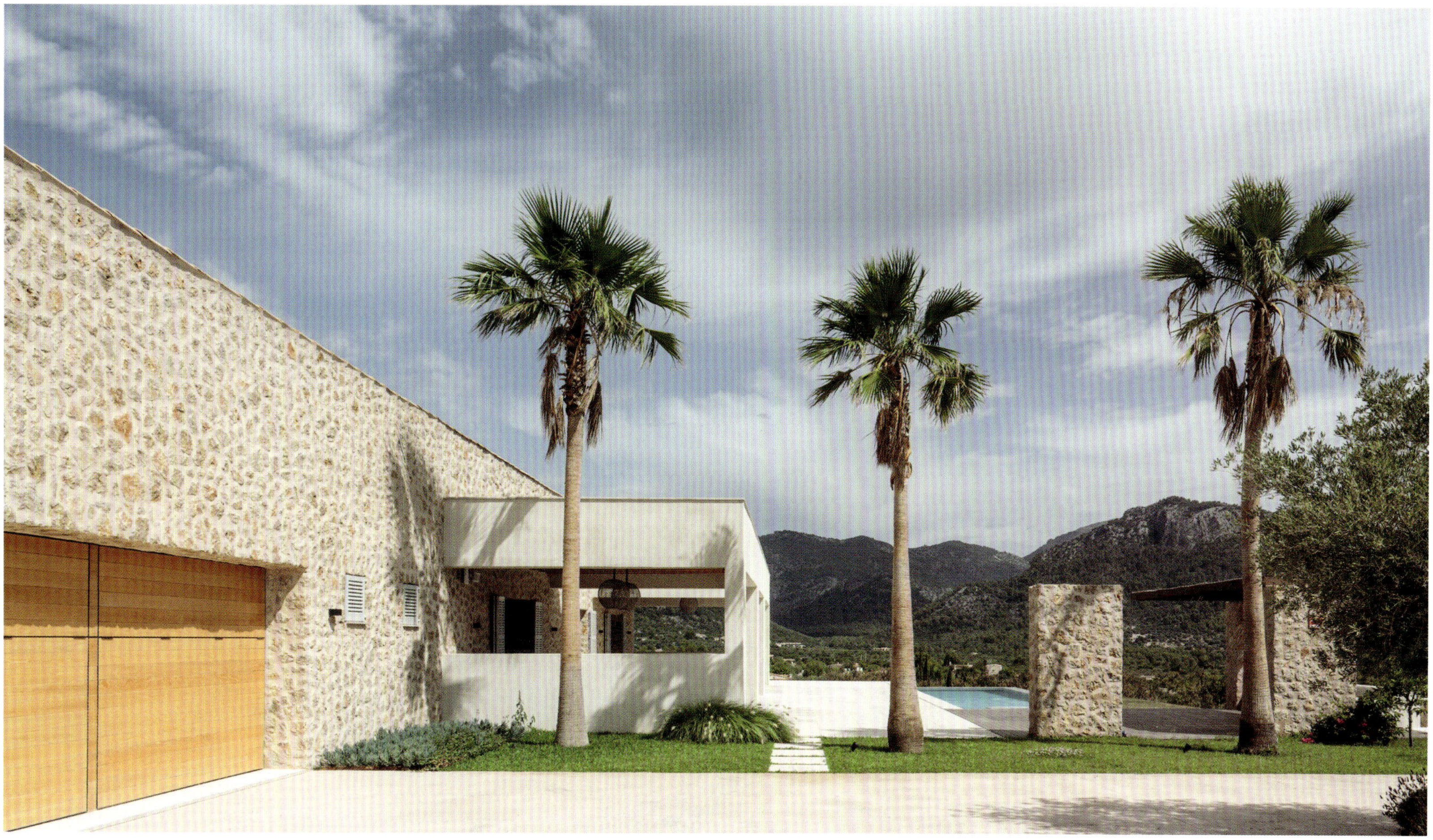

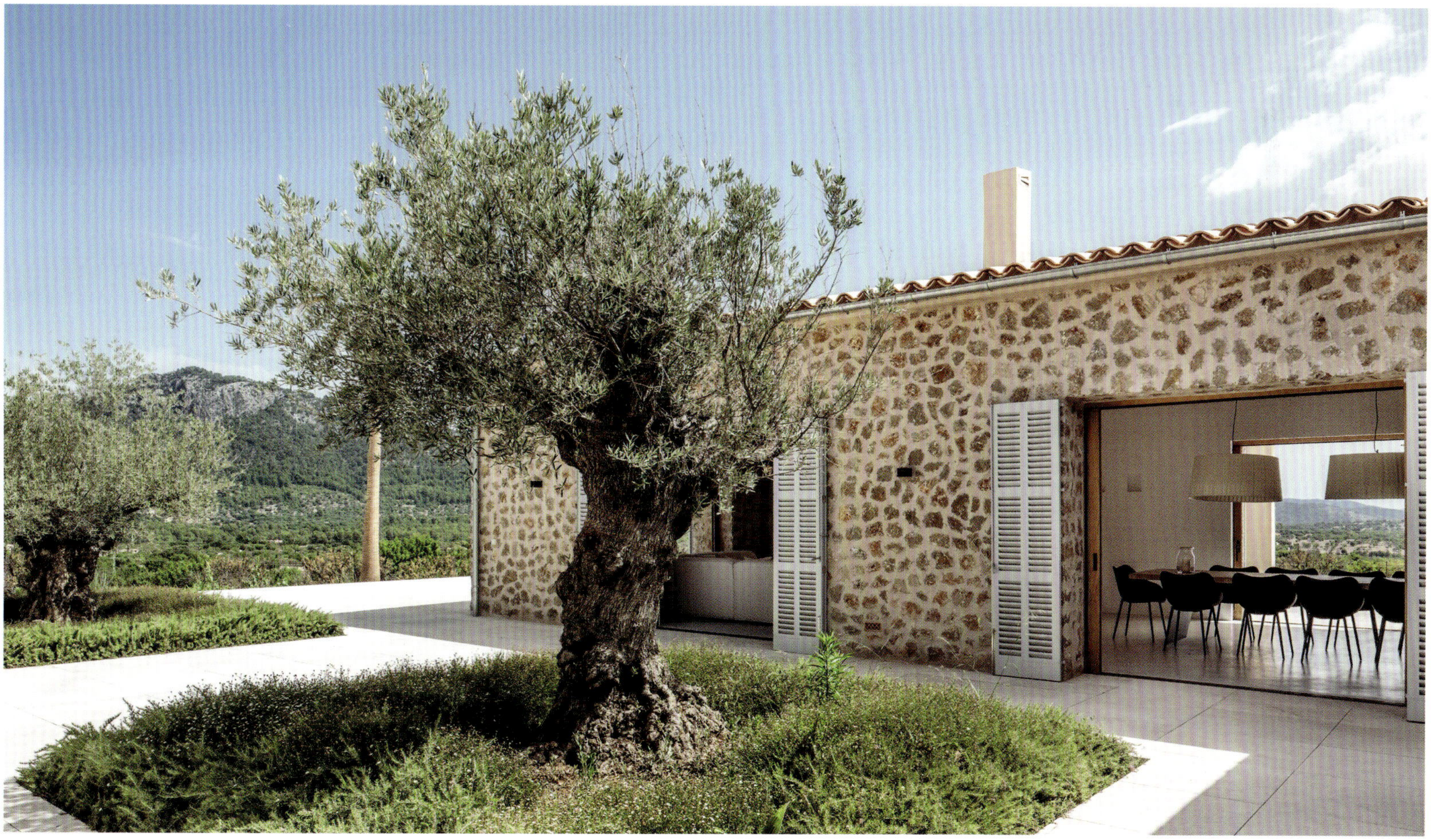

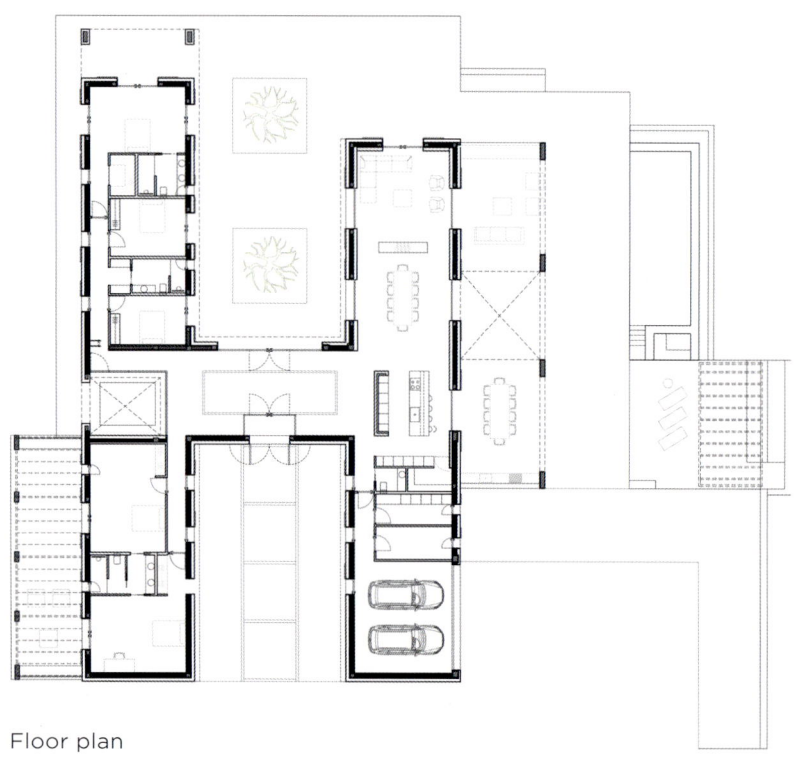

Floor plan

LOCAL MATERIALS SUCH AS NATURAL
STONE AND WOOD PRESERVE THE
LOCAL CHARACTER OF THE HOUSE

MORGAN
AND MORGAN

CALA CARBÓ

POLLENÇA

Located in Cala Carbó, an iconic coastal enclave in Mallorca, seven kilometers from Pollença, this three-story house with uninterrupted views of the Mediterranean Sea embodies the concept of slow living.
The property's gourmet kitchen has been designed not only as a space for cooking but also for relaxing and unwinding. The company Estils i Formes collaborated on the design under the direction of Pille Morgan. Custom-made furniture with walnut finishes includes extensive Italian stone countertops, while the handmade stone dining table serves as a central point for gatherings and dinners.
The main house combines on the ground floor the living-dining areas and kitchen with cream Zarci stone floors, whitewashed walls, and an integrated fireplace. The first floor houses two bedrooms, a bathroom with designer fixtures, and a private terrace with captivating sea views. The interior color palette in earthy tones complements the deep blue sea that enters through all the windows, creating a serene and relaxing atmosphere.

In Cala Carbó, einer ikonischen Küstenenklave auf Mallorca, sieben Kilometer von Pollença entfernt, verkörpert dieses dreistöckige Haus mit ununterbrochenem Blick auf das Mittelmeer das Konzept des langsamen Lebens.
Die Gourmetküche der Immobilie wurde nicht nur als Raum zum Kochen, sondern auch zum Entspannen und Abschalten entworfen. Das Unternehmen Estils i Formes arbeitete unter der Leitung von Pille Morgan an der Gestaltung mit. Maßgefertigte Möbel mit Walnussoberflächen umfassen ausgedehnte italienische Steinplatten, während der handgefertigte Steinesstisch als zentraler Punkt für Versammlungen und Abendessen dient.
Das Haupthaus kombiniert im Erdgeschoss die Wohn-Essbereiche und die Küche mit Böden aus cremefarbenem Zarci-Stein, weiß getünchten Wänden und einem integrierten Kamin. Im ersten Stock befinden sich zwei Schlafzimmer, ein Badezimmer mit Designer-Armaturen und eine private Terrasse mit faszinierendem Meerblick. Die Farbpalette im Inneren in Erdtönen ergänzt das tiefe Blau des Meeres, das durch alle Fenster hereinkommt, und schafft eine ruhige und entspannende Atmosphäre.

Située à Cala Carbó, une enclave côtière emblématique de Majorque, à sept kilomètres de Pollença, cette maison de trois étages avec vue imprenable sur la mer Méditerranée incarne le concept du slow living.
La cuisine gastronomique de la propriété a été conçue non seulement comme un espace pour cuisiner mais aussi pour se détendre et se déconnecter. La société Estils i Formes a collaboré à la conception sous la direction de Pille Morgan. Des meubles sur mesure avec des finitions en noyer incluent de vastes plans de travail en pierre italienne, tandis que la table à manger en pierre fabriquée à la main sert de point central pour les rassemblements et les dîners.
La maison principale combine au rez-de-chaussée les espaces de salon, salle à manger et cuisine avec des sols en pierre crème Zarci, des murs blanchis à la chaux et une cheminée intégrée. Le premier étage abrite deux chambres, une salle de bains avec des accessoires de designer et une terrasse privée avec des vues captivantes sur la mer. La palette de couleurs intérieures dans des tons terre s'harmonise avec le bleu profond de la mer qui entre par toutes les fenêtres, créant une atmosphère sereine et relaxante.

Situada en Cala Carbó, un icónico enclave costero de Mallorca a siete kilómetros de Pollença, esta vivienda de tres plantas y vistas ininterrumpidas del mar Mediterráneo, encarna el concepto del slow living.
La cocina gourmet de la propiedad ha sido diseñada no solo como un espacio para cocinar sino también para relajarse y desconectar. La empresa Estils i Formes colaboró en el diseño bajo la dirección de Pille Morgan. El mobiliario a medida con acabados de nogal incluye amplias encimeras de piedra italiana, mientras que la mesa de comedor de piedra hecha a mano se erige como un punto central para reuniones y cenas.
La casa principal combina en la planta baja las áreas de salón, comedor y cocina, con suelos de piedra crema zarci, paredes encaladas, y una chimenea integrada. La primera planta alberga dos dormitorios, un baño con accesorios de diseño y una terraza privada con vistas cautivadoras al mar. La paleta de colores en tonos tierra que domina en el interior, se acopla con el azul intenso del mar que entra por todas las ventanas, creando un ambiente sereno y relajante.

THE PROPERTY'S GOURMET KITCHEN IS DESIGNED FOR BOTH COOKING AND RELAXING

MY LANDSCAPING GROUP

SON PI

ARTÀ

Photos © Jens Boldt

FINCA BREEZE

LLUCMAJOR

Photos © Jens Boldt

This low-maintenance Mediterranean garden unfolds as a vibrant mosaic of colors where perennials intertwine with existing olive and mulberry trees, creating shade and structure in the space. The landscaper Johannes Duetsch designed this garden to complement a rustic estate built by Moredesign. The 28,500 m² area has been divided with low dry-stone walls to create terraces connected by stone slabs and lippia nodiflora, a ground cover plant species. Upon arrival at the estate, a parterre welcomes visitors with a majestic olive tree surrounded by stipa tenuissima, known as "pony tails," which adds movement and texture. Around the pool, patches of lilac and purple *perovskia atriplicifolia* (Russian sage) and agapanthus create an impressive visual effect. The orchard and interior courtyard have also been enriched with citrus, aromatic herbs, and jasmine selected for their sustainability and ability to attract beneficial insects. The garden's design integrates with the natural landscape of the UNESCO-recognized environment and blends with the architecture of the family home, creating a continuous and romantic atmosphere that invites enjoyment of every corner.

Dieser pflegeleichte mediterrane Garten entfaltet sich wie ein lebendiges Mosaik aus Farben, in dem mehrjährige Pflanzen mit den vorhandenen Oliven- und Maulbeerbäumen verschmelzen und Schatten und Struktur im Raum schaffen. Der Landschaftsgestalter Johannes Duetsch entwarf diesen Garten, um ein rustikales Anwesen zu ergänzen, das von Moredesign gebaut wurde. Die 28.500 Quadratmeter große Fläche wurde mit niedrigen Trockensteinmauern unterteilt, um Terrassen zu schaffen, die durch Steinplatten und Lippia nodiflora, eine Bodendeckerpflanze, miteinander verbunden sind. Bei der Ankunft auf dem Anwesen empfängt ein Parterre die Besucher mit einem majestätischen Olivenbaum, der von stipa tenuissima, bekannt als „pony tails", umgeben ist und Bewegung und Textur hinzufügt. Um den Pool schaffen Flecken aus lila und violetter *perovskia atriplicifolia* (russischer Salbei) und Agapanthus einen beeindruckenden visuellen Effekt. Der Obstgarten und der Innenhof wurden ebenfalls mit Zitrusbäumen, aromatischen Kräutern und Jasmin bereichert, die aufgrund ihrer Nachhaltigkeit und ihrer Fähigkeit, nützliche Insekten anzuziehen, ausgewählt wurden. Das Design des Gartens integriert sich in die natürliche Landschaft des von der UNESCO anerkannten Umfelds und verschmilzt mit der Architektur des Familienhauses, wodurch eine kontinuierliche und romantische Atmosphäre entsteht, die zum Genuss jedes Winkels einlädt.

Ce jardin méditerranéen à faible consommation se déploie comme une mosaïque vibrante de couleurs où les plantes vivaces s'entrelacent avec les oliviers et mûriers existants, créant de l'ombre et de la structure dans l'espace. Le paysagiste Johannes Duetsch a conçu ce jardin pour compléter une propriété rustique construite par Moredesign. Les 28 500 mètres carrés de surface ont été divisés avec des murs bas en pierre sèche pour créer des terrasses reliées par des dalles de pierre et la lippia nodiflora, une espèce de plante couvre-sol. À l'arrivée à la propriété, un parterre accueille les visiteurs avec un majestueux olivier entouré de stipa tenuissima, connue sous le nom de « pony tails », apportant mouvement et texture. Autour de la piscine, des taches de couleurs lilas et violettes de *perovskia atriplicifolia* (sauge russe) et d'agapanthes créent un effet visuel impressionnant. Le verger et la cour intérieure ont également été enrichis de citronniers, d'herbes aromatiques et de jasmins choisis pour leur durabilité et leur capacité à attirer des insectes bénéfiques. Le design du jardin s'intègre au paysage naturel de l'environnement reconnu par l'UNESCO et se fond avec l'architecture de la maison familiale, créant une atmosphère continue et romantique qui invite à profiter de chaque recoin.

Este jardín mediterráneo de bajo consumo se despliega como un vibrante mosaico de colores, donde las plantas perennes se entrelazan con olivos y moreras preexistentes, creando sombra y estructura en el espacio. El paisajista Johannes Duetsch, ha diseñado este jardín que complementa una finca rústica construida por Moredesign. Los 28.500 metros cuadrados de superficie se han dividido con muros bajos de piedra seca, para crear terrazas conectadas por senderos de losetas y lippia nodiflora, una especie de planta tapizante. Al llegar a la finca, un parterre recibe a los visitantes con un majestuoso olivo rodeado de stipa tenuissima, conocida como esparto «pony tails», que aporta movimiento y textura. Alrededor de la piscina, las manchas de colores lilas y morados de la *perovskia atriplicifolia* (salvia rusa) y los Agapantos crean un efecto visual impresionante. El huerto y el patio interior también se han enriquecido con cítricos, hierbas aromáticas y jazmines, seleccionados por su sostenibilidad y su capacidad para atraer insectos beneficiosos. El diseño del jardín se integra con el paisaje natural del entorno reconocido por la UNESCO, y confluye con la arquitectura de la casa familiar, creando un ambiente continuo y romántico que invita a disfrutar de cada rincón.

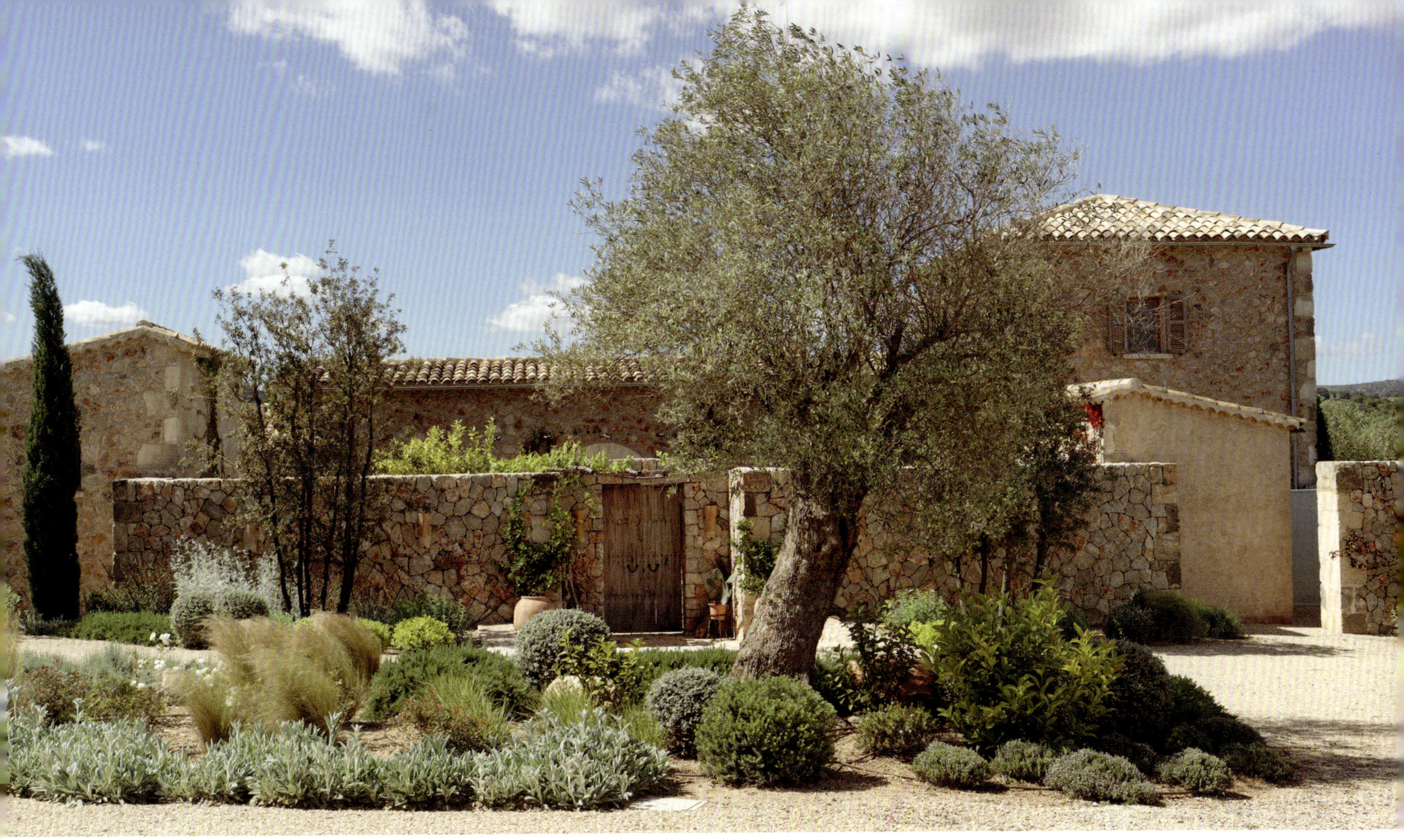

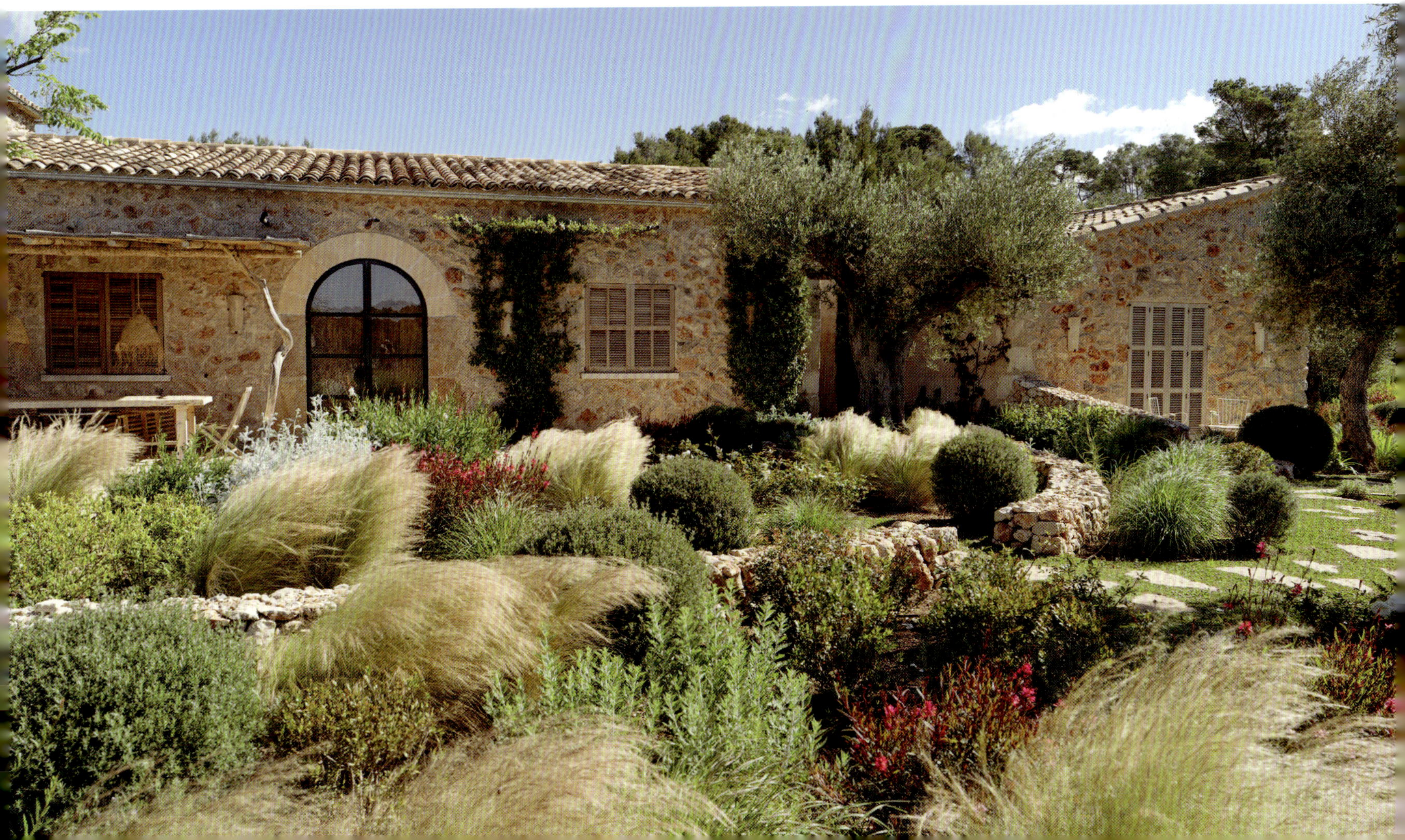

A house over three centuries old, built with solid stone and an underground well, has been converted into a self-sufficient dwelling. Originally divided into two by the family's patriarch, the property included an annex area bounded by a natural stone wall where farm animals used to reside, protected by prickly pear cacti. The renovation of this area resulted in a cozy guest residence with a pergola under the shade of a native olive tree. Additionally, water self-sufficiency was achieved thanks to the well and energy self-sufficiency through solar panels and lithium batteries. The garden has been designed to maximize comfort and relaxation with rest corners and loungers lining the terrace and pool. Different environments were created, from tropical areas with rain showers to classic Mediterranean gardens with olive trees, lavender, rosemary, and rolling lawns. Sustainability has been a key factor, from the selection of fruit and citrus trees to the creation of a vegetable garden, seeking to maintain balance with the natural environment. This former animal house has been transformed into a modern and eco-friendly home.

Ein über drei Jahrhunderte altes Haus, gebaut aus massivem Stein und mit einem unterirdischen Brunnen, wurde in ein autarkes Wohnhaus umgewandelt. Ursprünglich vom Familienpatriarchen in zwei Teile geteilt, umfasste das Anwesen einen Anbau, der von einer Natursteinmauer umgeben war, in dem früher Nutztiere untergebracht waren, geschützt von Feigenkakteen. Die Renovierung dieses Bereichs führte zu einer gemütlichen Gästeresidenz mit einer Pergola unter dem Schatten eines einheimischen Olivenbaums. Darüber hinaus wurde die Wasserselbstversorgung durch den Brunnen und die Energieselbstversorgung durch Solarpaneele und Lithiumbatterien erreicht. Der Garten wurde so gestaltet, dass er maximalen Komfort und Entspannung bietet, mit Ruheplätzen und Liegestühlen entlang der Terrasse und des Pools. Es wurden verschiedene Umgebungen geschaffen, von tropischen Bereichen mit Regenduschen bis hin zu klassischen mediterranen Gärten mit Olivenbäumen, Lavendel, Rosmarin und weitläufigen Rasenflächen. Nachhaltigkeit war ein Schlüsselfaktor, von der Auswahl der Obst- und Zitrusbäume bis hin zur Schaffung eines Gemüsegartens, wobei versucht wurde, das Gleichgewicht mit der natürlichen Umgebung zu bewahren. Dieses ehemalige Tierhaus wurde in ein modernes und umweltfreundliches Zuhause verwandelt.

Une maison de plus de trois siècles, construite en pierre solide et avec un puits souterrain, a été convertie en une habitation autosuffisante. Originellement divisée en deux par le patriarche de la famille, la propriété comprenait une zone annexe délimitée par un mur en pierre naturelle où résidaient les animaux de la ferme, protégés par des cactus de figuier de Barbarie. La rénovation de cette zone a abouti à une résidence d'invités accueillante avec une pergola sous l'ombre d'un olivier natif. De plus, l'autosuffisance en eau a été réalisée grâce au puits et l'autosuffisance énergétique grâce aux panneaux solaires et aux batteries au lithium. Le jardin a été conçu pour maximiser le confort et la détente avec des coins de repos et des chaises longues bordant la terrasse et la piscine. Différents environnements ont été créés, des zones tropicales avec des douches de pluie aux jardins méditerranéens classiques avec des oliviers, de la lavande, du romarin et des pelouses ondulantes. La durabilité a été un facteur clé, depuis la sélection des arbres fruitiers et des agrumes jusqu'à la création d'un potager, cherchant à maintenir l'équilibre avec l'environnement naturel. Cette ancienne maison d'animaux a été transformée en une habitation moderne et écologique.

Una casa de más de tres siglos, construida con piedra sólida y con un pozo subterráneo, ha sido reconvertida en una vivienda autosuficiente. Originalmente dividida en dos por el patriarca de la familia, la propiedad contaba con un área anexa delimitada por un muro de piedra natural, donde solían residir los animales de granja, protegidos por cactus de higo chumbo. La renovación de esta zona derivó en una acogedora residencia para huéspedes, con una pérgola bajo la sombra de un olivo nativo. Además, se logró la autosuficiencia hídrica gracias al pozo, y la energética a través de paneles solares y baterías de litio. El jardín se ha diseñado para maximizar el confort y la distensión, con rincones de descanso y tumbonas que bordean la terraza y la piscina. Se crearon diferentes ambientes, desde zonas tropicales con duchas de lluvia, hasta jardines mediterráneos clásicos con olivos, lavanda, romero y campos de césped ondulantes. La sostenibilidad ha sido un factor clave, desde la elección de árboles frutales y cítricos, hasta la creación de un huerto de vegetales, buscando mantener el equilibrio con el entorno natural. Esta antigua casa de animales se ha transformado en una vivienda moderna y ecológica.

SUSTAINABILITY IS A KEY FACTOR
IN THIS DWELLING

OHLAB

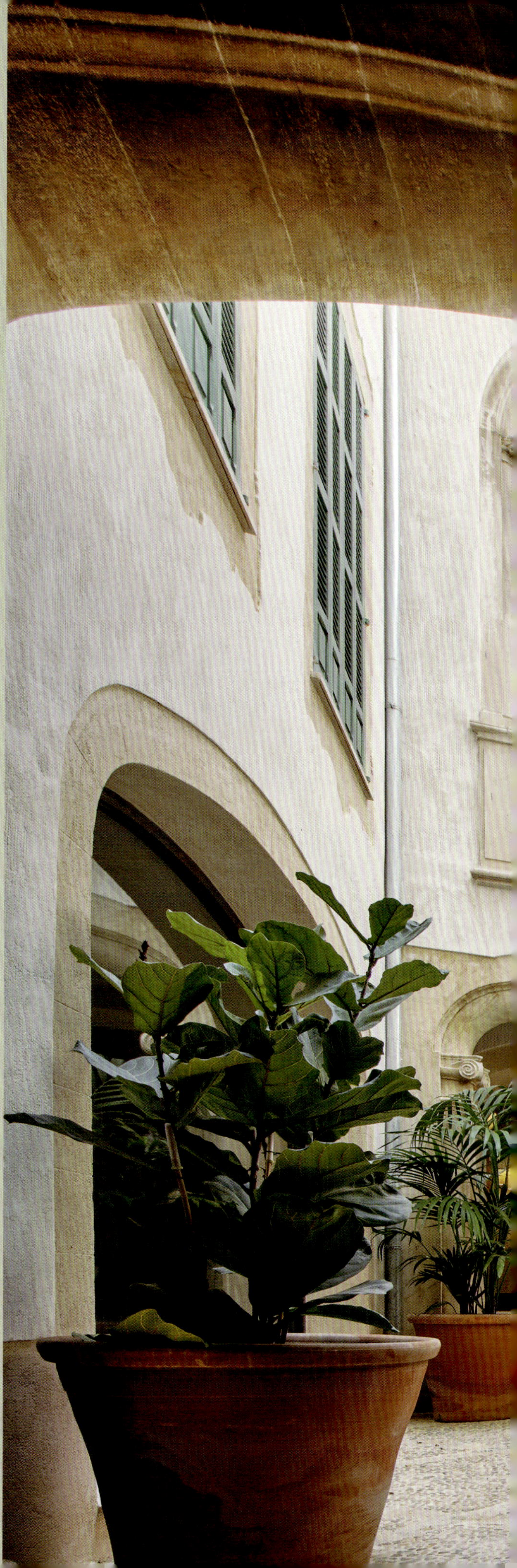

CAN SANTACILIA

PALMA DE MALLORCA

Photos © José Hevia

In the historic heart of Palma de Mallorca stands Can Santacilia, a rehabilitation of two buildings converted into an exclusive residential complex. The final result addresses and accounts for the numerous modifications these 12th and 13th-century constructions have undergone. The challenge was to create a modern and comfortable residential building by integrating the complex and fragmented original structure with a protected 16th-century façade and volume. The architects took advantage of this situation to give each residence individualized solutions, articulating them with the new common areas.

Natural, noble, and local materials emphasize the Mediterranean identity. Alongside the restoration of historical elements, new high-quality materials were introduced, such as antique bronze, porcelain, local stones, and details of linen and cotton textiles. The main courtyard is the entrance that connects with the landscaped terraces and common areas, such as a gym and an indoor pool with a spa. Special attention has been paid to sustainability throughout all processes. The result is a work that balances historical essence and contemporaneity.

Im historischen Herzen von Palma de Mallorca steht Can Santacilia, eine Rehabilitation von zwei Gebäuden, die in einen exklusiven Wohnkomplex umgewandelt wurden. Das Endergebnis berücksichtigt die zahlreichen Modifikationen, die diese Bauten aus dem 12. und 13. Jahrhundert erfahren haben. Die Herausforderung bestand darin, ein modernes und komfortables Wohngebäude zu schaffen, indem die komplexe und fragmentierte Originalstruktur mit einer geschützten Fassade und einem Volumen aus dem 16. Jahrhundert integriert wurde. Die Architekten nutzten diese Situation, um jeder Wohnung individuelle Lösungen zu geben und sie mit den neuen Gemeinschaftsbereichen zu verbinden.

Natürliche, edle und lokale Materialien betonen die mediterrane Identität. Neben der Restaurierung historischer Elemente wurden neue hochwertige Materialien wie antikes Bronze, Porzellan, lokale Steine und Details aus Leinen- und Baumwolltextilien eingeführt. Der Haupthof ist der Eingang, der mit den gestalteten Terrassen und Gemeinschaftsbereichen wie einem Fitnessstudio und einem Innenpool mit Spa verbindet. Besonderes Augenmerk wurde auf Nachhaltigkeit in allen Prozessen gelegt. Das Ergebnis ist ein Werk, das historische Essenz und Zeitgenossenschaft in Einklang bringt.

Au cœur historique de Palma de Majorque se dresse Can Santacilia, une réhabilitation de deux bâtiments convertis en un complexe résidentiel exclusif. Le résultat final aborde et prend en compte les nombreuses modifications subies par ces constructions des XIIe et XIIIe siècles. Le défi était de créer un bâtiment résidentiel moderne et confortable en intégrant la structure originale complexe et fragmentée avec une façade et un volume protégés du XVIe siècle. Les architectes ont profité de cette situation pour donner à chaque logement des solutions individualisées, les articulant avec les nouvelles zones communes.

Les matériaux naturels, nobles et locaux soulignent l'identité méditerranéenne. Aux côtés de la restauration d'éléments historiques, de nouveaux matériaux de haute qualité ont été introduits, tels que le bronze ancien, la porcelaine, les pierres locales et les détails de textiles en lin et coton. La cour principale est l'entrée qui relie aux terrasses paysagées et aux zones communes telles qu'un gymnase et une piscine intérieure avec spa. Une attention particulière a été portée à la durabilité dans tous les processus. Le résultat est une œuvre qui équilibre l'essence historique et la contemporanéité.

En el corazón histórico de Palma de Mallorca se alza Can Santacilia, una rehabilitación de dos edificios convertidos en un exclusivo conjunto residencial. El resultado final aborda y da cuenta de las numerosas modificaciones sufridas por estas construcciones de los siglos XII y XIII. El desafío fue crear un edificio residencial moderno y confortable, integrando la estructura original, compleja y fragmentada, con una fachada y volumen protegidos del siglo XVI. Los arquitectos aprovecharon esta situación dar a cada vivienda soluciones individualizadas, articulándolas con las nuevas áreas comunes.

Los materiales naturales, nobles y locales enfatizan la identidad mediterránea. Junto a la restauración de elementos históricos se introdujeron nuevos materiales de calidad, como bronce antiguo, porcelana, piedras locales y detalles de textiles de lino y algodón. El patio principal es la entrada que conecta con las terrazas ajardinadas y las áreas comunes como un gimnasio y una piscina cubierta con spa. En todos los procesos se ha puesto especial atención a la sostenibilidad. El resultado es una obra que equilibra la esencia histórica y la contemporaneidad.

NATURAL NOBLE AND LOCAL
MATERIALS EMPHASIZE THE
MEDITERRANEAN IDENTITY

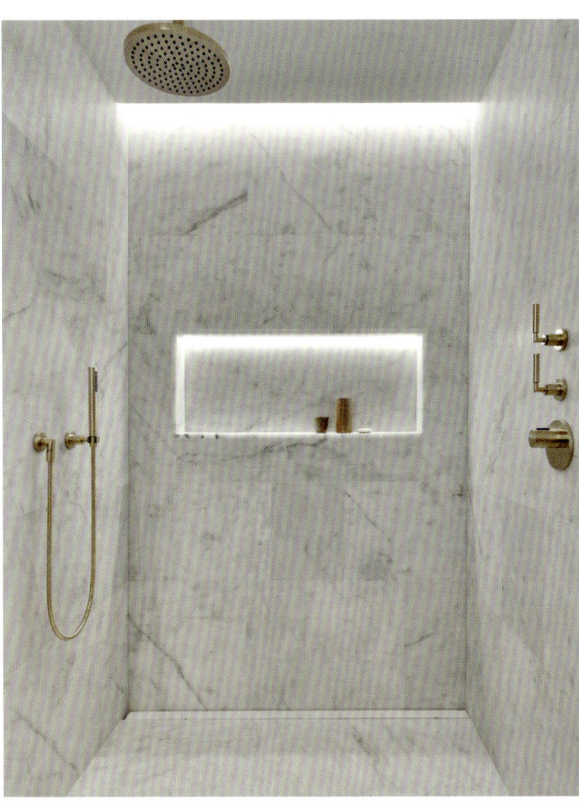

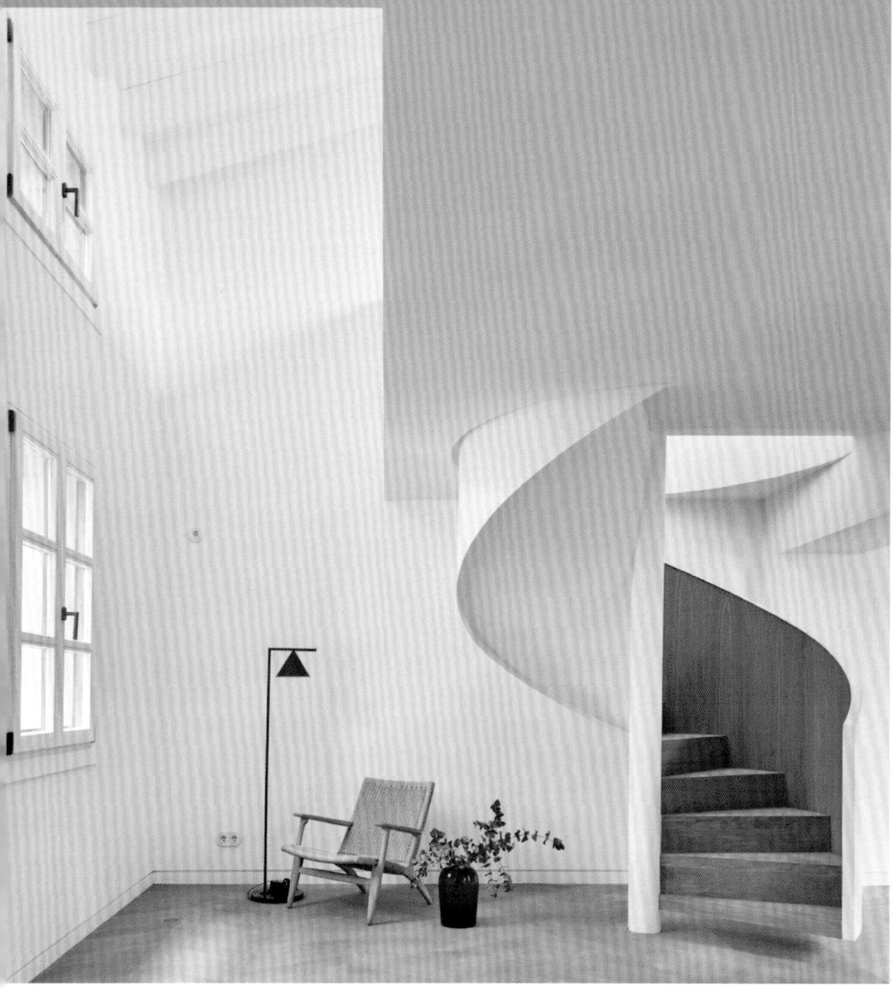
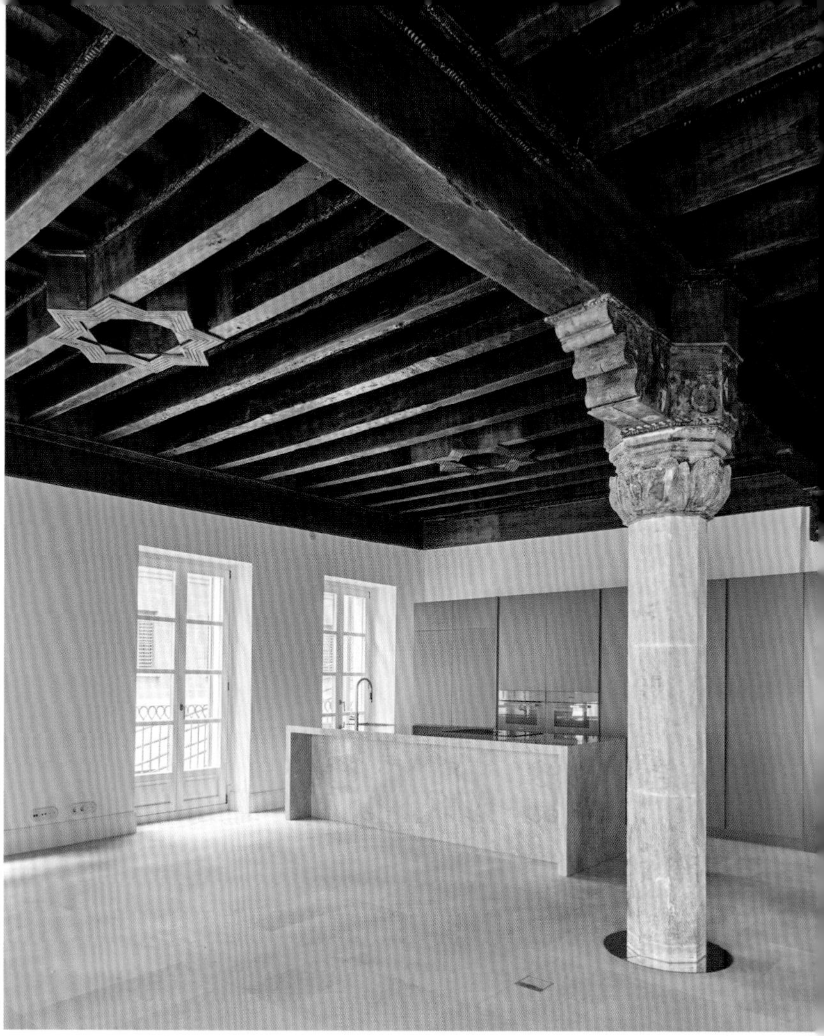
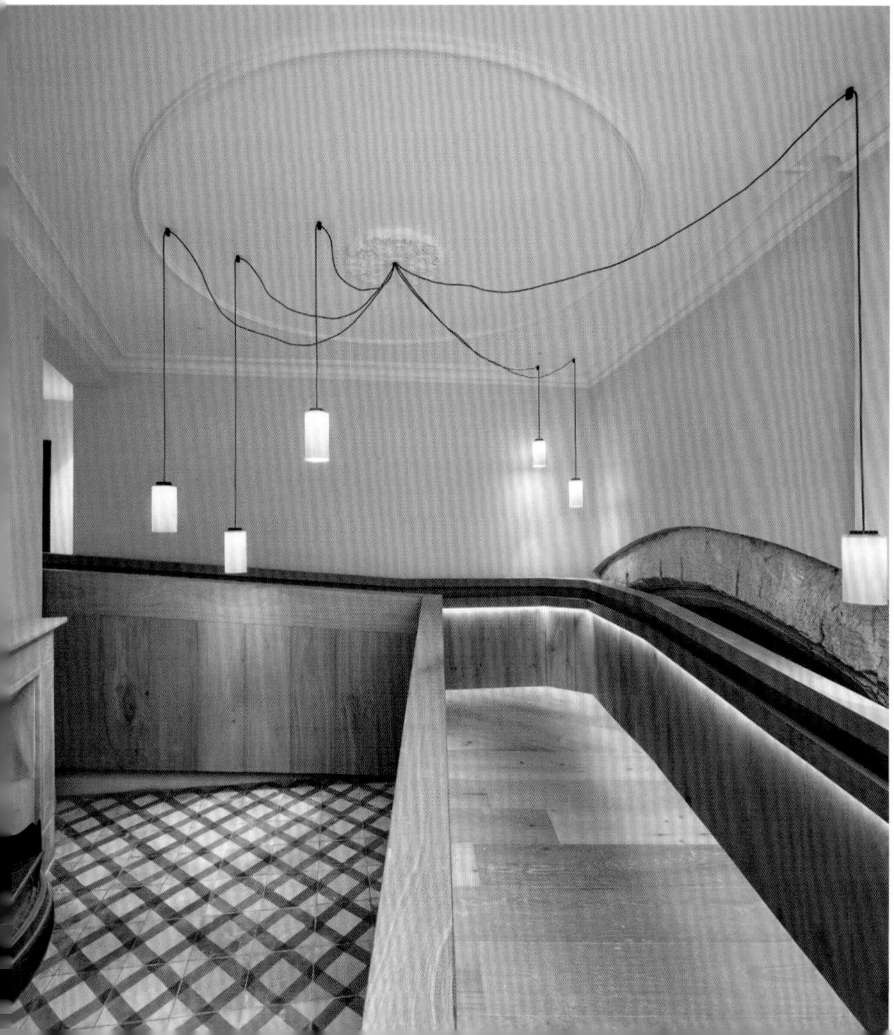
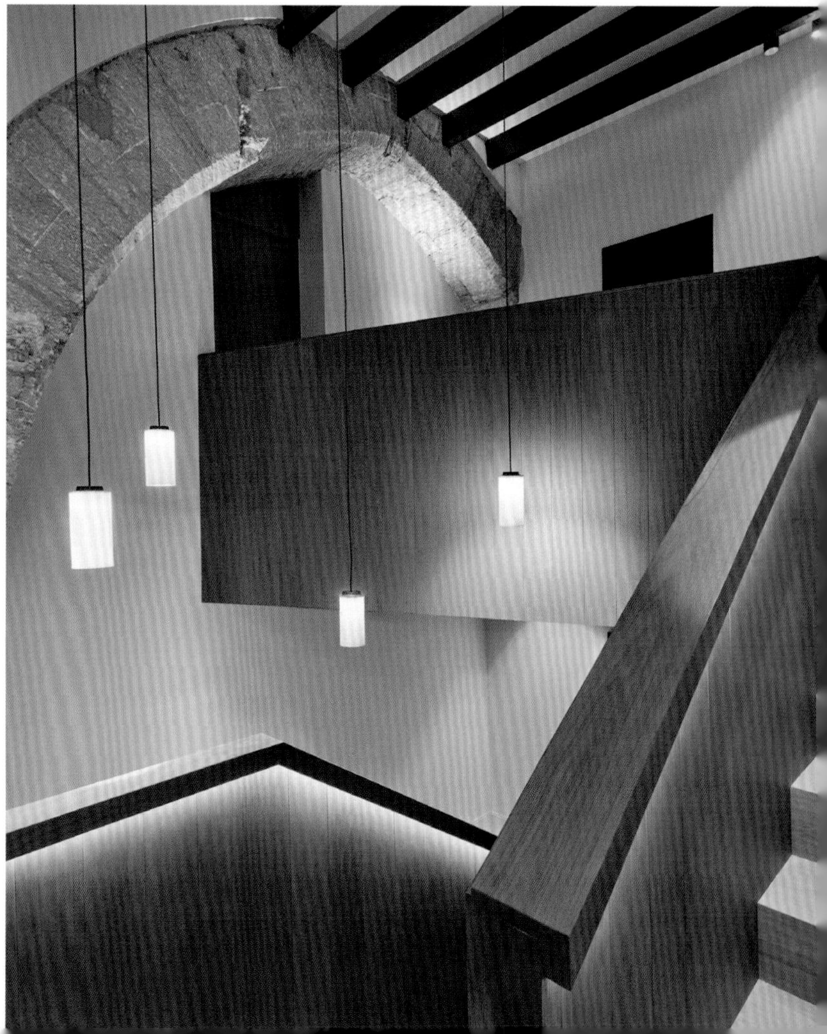

PORTELL DESIGN &
CONSTRUCTION

VERDEROL

PORT D'ANDRATX

Photos © Tomeu Canyelles

Among pines and the sea lies this renovated house with views of Dragonera island. The property, adapted to the rugged geography of the terrain, is distributed over three levels with a Mediterranean identity reflected in all elements of the renovation project.
The façade stands out for its dry stone walls typical of the island, combined with white wooden beams and Binissalem stone floors. Inside, ceilings with more recovered wooden beams and large windows open the house to the garden and sea. The use of local materials creates a light atmosphere that integrates rustic elements such as panel windows with more modern ones like continuous micro-cement floors. The furniture is a combination of custom-made pieces. Linen sofas, beds with jute headboards, and reclaimed pieces maintain the constant use of natural materials. In the kitchen and bathrooms, river stone has been worked with micro-cement floors. Binissalem stone countertops accompany custom-made oak furniture. The renovation has brought luminosity and new life to the house, respecting its Mediterranean essence and making the most of the views and natural surroundings.

Zwischen Kiefern und dem Meer liegt dieses renovierte Haus mit Blick auf die Insel Dragonera. Das Anwesen, das an die zerklüftete Geographie des Geländes angepasst ist, erstreckt sich über drei Ebenen mit einer mediterranen Identität, die sich in allen Elementen des Renovierungsprojekts widerspiegelt.
Die Fassade zeichnet sich durch ihre Trockensteinmauern aus, die typisch für die Insel sind und mit weißen Holzbalken und Böden aus Binissalem-Stein kombiniert wurden. Innen öffnen sich Decken mit wiederverwendeten Holzbalken und großen Fenstern das Haus zum Garten und Meer. Die Verwendung lokaler Materialien schafft eine leichte Atmosphäre, die rustikale Elemente wie Paneelfenster mit moderneren wie kontinuierlichen Mikrozementböden integriert. Die Möbel sind eine Kombination aus maßgefertigten Stücken. Leinen-Sofas, Betten mit Jute-Kopfenden und wiederverwendete Stücke erhalten die konstante Verwendung natürlicher Materialien. In der Küche und den Badezimmern wurde Flussstein mit Mikrozementböden verarbeitet. Arbeitsplatten aus Binissalem-Stein begleiten maßgefertigte Eichenmöbel. Die Renovierung brachte Helligkeit und neues Leben in das Haus, respektierte seine mediterrane Essenz und nutzte die Aussicht und die natürliche Umgebung optimal.

Parmi les pins et la mer se trouve cette maison rénovée avec vue sur l'île de Dragonera. La propriété, adaptée à la géographie escarpée du terrain, est répartie sur trois niveaux avec une identité méditerranéenne reflétée dans tous les éléments du projet de rénovation.
La façade se distingue par ses murs en pierre sèche typiques de l'île, combinés avec des poutres en bois blanc et des sols en pierre de Binissalem. À l'intérieur, des plafonds avec des poutres en bois récupérées et de grandes fenêtres ouvrent la maison sur le jardin et la mer. L'utilisation de matériaux locaux crée une atmosphère légère qui intègre des éléments rustiques tels que les fenêtres à carreaux avec d'autres plus modernes comme les sols en microciment continu. Le mobilier est une combinaison de pièces faites sur mesure. Des canapés en lin, des lits avec des têtes de lit en jute et des pièces récupérées maintiennent l'utilisation constante de matériaux naturels. Dans la cuisine et les salles de bains, le galet a été travaillé avec des sols en microciment. Les plans de travail en Binissalem accompagnent les meubles sur mesure en chêne. La rénovation a apporté de la luminosité et une nouvelle vie à la maison, respectant son essence méditerranéenne et tirant le meilleur parti des vues et de l'environnement naturel.

Entre pinos y mar se encuentra esta vivienda renovada con vistas a la isla Dragonera. La propiedad, adaptada a la escarpada geografía del terreno, se distribuye en tres niveles con una identidad mediterránea que se refleja en todos los elementos del proyecto de reforma.
La fachada destaca por sus paredes de piedra en seco, típicas de la isla, combinadas con vigas de madera blanca y suelos de piedra de Binissalem. En el interior, techos con más vigas de madera recuperada y grandes ventanales abren la vivienda al jardín y al mar. A través del uso de materiales locales, se crea una atmósfera ligera que integra elementos rústicos, como las ventanas de cuarterones, con otros más modernos, como los suelos continuos de microcemento. El mobiliario es una combinación de piezas hechas a medida. Sofás de lino, camas con cabezales de yute y piezas recuperadas mantienen la constante de los materiales naturales. En la cocina y los baños, se ha trabajado el canto rodado con suelos de microcemento. Encimeras de Binissalem acompañan los muebles a medida en roble. La reforma ha aportado luminosidad y una nueva vida a la vivienda, respetando su esencia mediterránea y aprovechando al máximo las vistas y el entorno natural.

LOCAL MATERIALS BLEND RUSTIC PANEL WINDOWS WITH MODERN
MICRO-CEMENT FLOORS, CREATING A UNIFIED, LIGHT ATMOSPHERE

PS ARQUITECTOS + MARGA COMAS INTERIOR DESIGN

SANTANYÍ

SANTANYÍ

Photos © David Vega, Xisco Kamal

In the heart of the picturesque old town of Santanyí, this house is the result of a remarkable transformation thanks to the joint work of PS Arquitectos and Marga Comas in interior design.
Originally composed of two volumes, one residential and the other dedicated to agricultural activities, the building faced serious structural challenges after years of neglect. Faced with this scenario, it was decided to carry out a complete demolition, giving way to a reconstruction of the volumes. The former agricultural space was completely transformed into a spacious and bright living area with a kitchen and dining room. Two generous windows were opened to the exterior patio, and a marés stone arch—a typical sandstone of the island—was preserved as a balcony over the main room of the house. The interior courtyard features a dark-bottomed pool over which water falls like a fountain. In the interiors, the original stone walls contrast with other pure white walls. The selection of woods and the incorporation of three levels along with a lightbox bring the interior spaces to life, flooding them with a warm luminosity.

Im Herzen der malerischen Altstadt von Santanyí ist dieses Haus das Ergebnis einer bemerkenswerten Transformation durch die gemeinsame Arbeit von PS Arquitectos und Marga Comas im Innendesign.
Ursprünglich bestehend aus zwei Volumen, einem Wohnbereich und dem anderen für landwirtschaftliche Aktivitäten, stand das Gebäude nach Jahren der Vernachlässigung vor ernsthaften strukturellen Herausforderungen. Angesichts dieses Szenarios wurde beschlossen, eine vollständige Abriss zu vollziehen und den Wiederaufbau der Volumen vorzunehmen. Der ehemalige landwirtschaftliche Raum wurde vollständig in einen geräumigen und hellen Wohnbereich mit Küche und Esszimmer umgewandelt. Zwei großzügige Fenster wurden zum Außenhof geöffnet, und ein Marés-Bogen - ein typischer Sandstein der Insel - wurde als Balkon über dem Hauptraum des Hauses bewahrt. Der Innenhof verfügt über einen dunklen Pool, über den Wasser wie ein Brunnen fließt. Im Inneren kontrastieren die ursprünglichen Steinmauern mit anderen reinen weißen Wänden. Die Auswahl der Hölzer und die Integration von drei Ebenen sowie einer Lichtbox bringen Leben in die Innenräume und fluten sie mit einer warmen Helligkeit.

Au cœur du pittoresque centre historique de Santanyí, cette maison est le résultat d'une transformation remarquable grâce au travail conjoint de PS Arquitectos et Marga Comas en design intérieur.
Initialement composée de deux volumes, l'un résidentiel et l'autre dédié aux activités agricoles, le bâtiment faisait face à de sérieux défis structurels après des années de négligence. Face à ce scénario, il a été décidé de procéder à une démolition complète, laissant place à une reconstruction des volumes. L'ancien espace agricole a été entièrement transformé en un espace de vie spacieux et lumineux avec une cuisine et une salle à manger. Deux grandes fenêtres ont été ouvertes sur le patio extérieur, et une arche en marés - une pierre calcaire typique de l'île - a été préservée en tant que balcon sur la pièce principale de la maison. Le patio intérieur dispose d'une piscine à fond sombre sur laquelle tombe de l'eau comme une fontaine. À l'intérieur, les murs en pierre d'origine contrastent avec d'autres murs d'un blanc pur. La sélection des bois et l'incorporation de trois niveaux ainsi qu'une boîte à lumière donnent vie aux espaces intérieurs, les inondant d'une luminosité chaleureuse.

En el corazón del pintoresco casco antiguo de Santanyí, esta casa es el resultado de una notable transformación gracias al trabajo conjunto de PS Arquitectos y Marga Comas en el diseño interior.
Originalmente compuesta por dos volúmenes, uno habitacional y otro dedicado a actividades agrícolas, el edificio enfrentaba serios desafíos estructurales tras años de abandono. Ante este escenario, se tomó la decisión de llevar a cabo una demolición integral, dando paso a una reconstrucción de los volúmenes. Se transformó por completo el antiguo espacio agrícola, convirtiéndolo en un amplio y luminoso espacio de estar con cocina y comedor. Se abrieron dos generosos ventanales hacia el patio exterior, y se preservó un arco de Marés, típica piedra arenisca de la isla, a modo de balcón sobre la estancia principal de la vivienda. El patio interior cuenta con una piscina de fondo oscuro sobre el que cae agua a modo de fuente. En los interiores predominan las paredes de piedra originales, en contraste con otras paredes en blanco puro. La selección de maderas y la incorporación de tres alturas, junto con una caja de luz, dan vida a los espacios interiores, inundándolos de una cálida luminosidad.

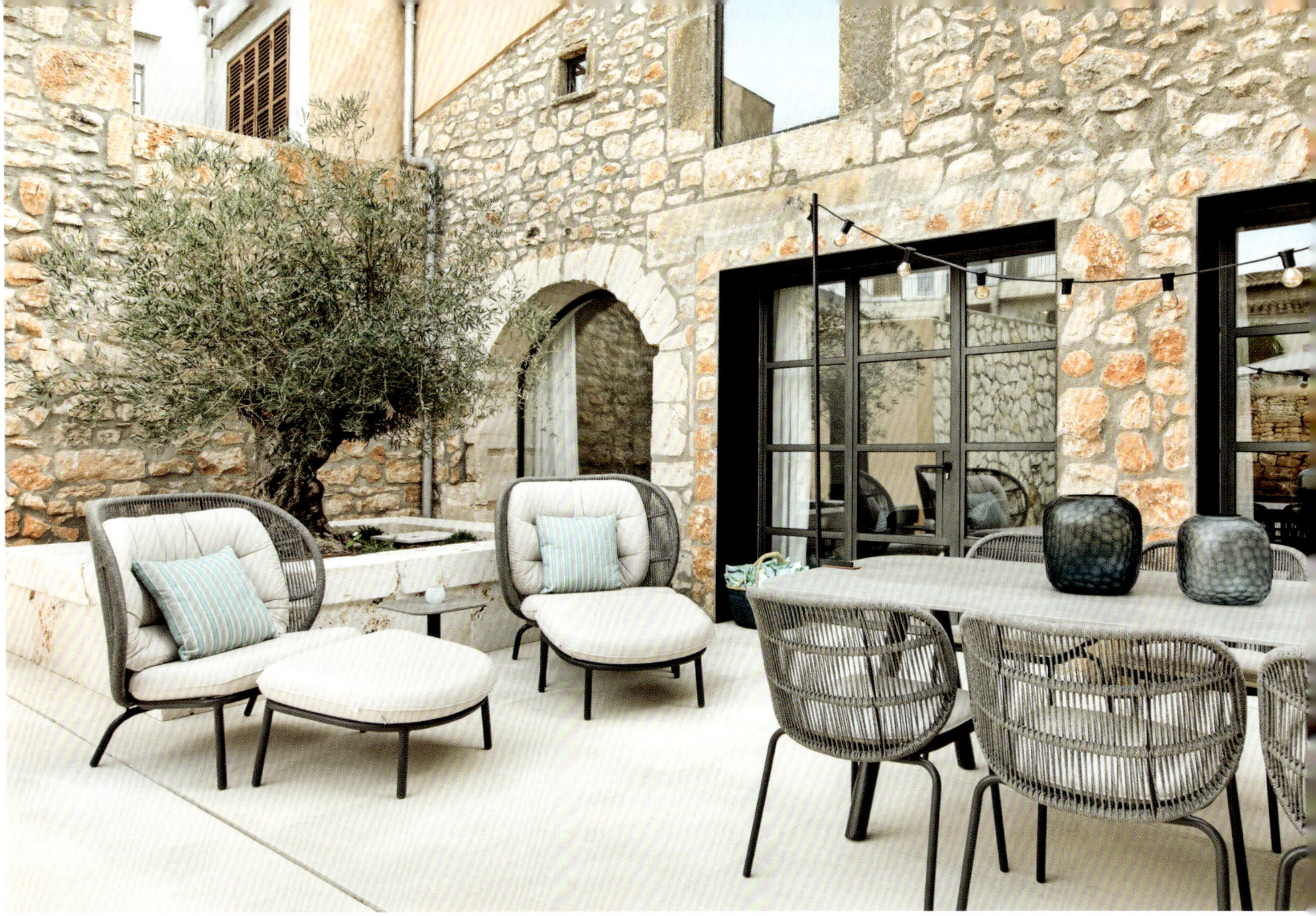

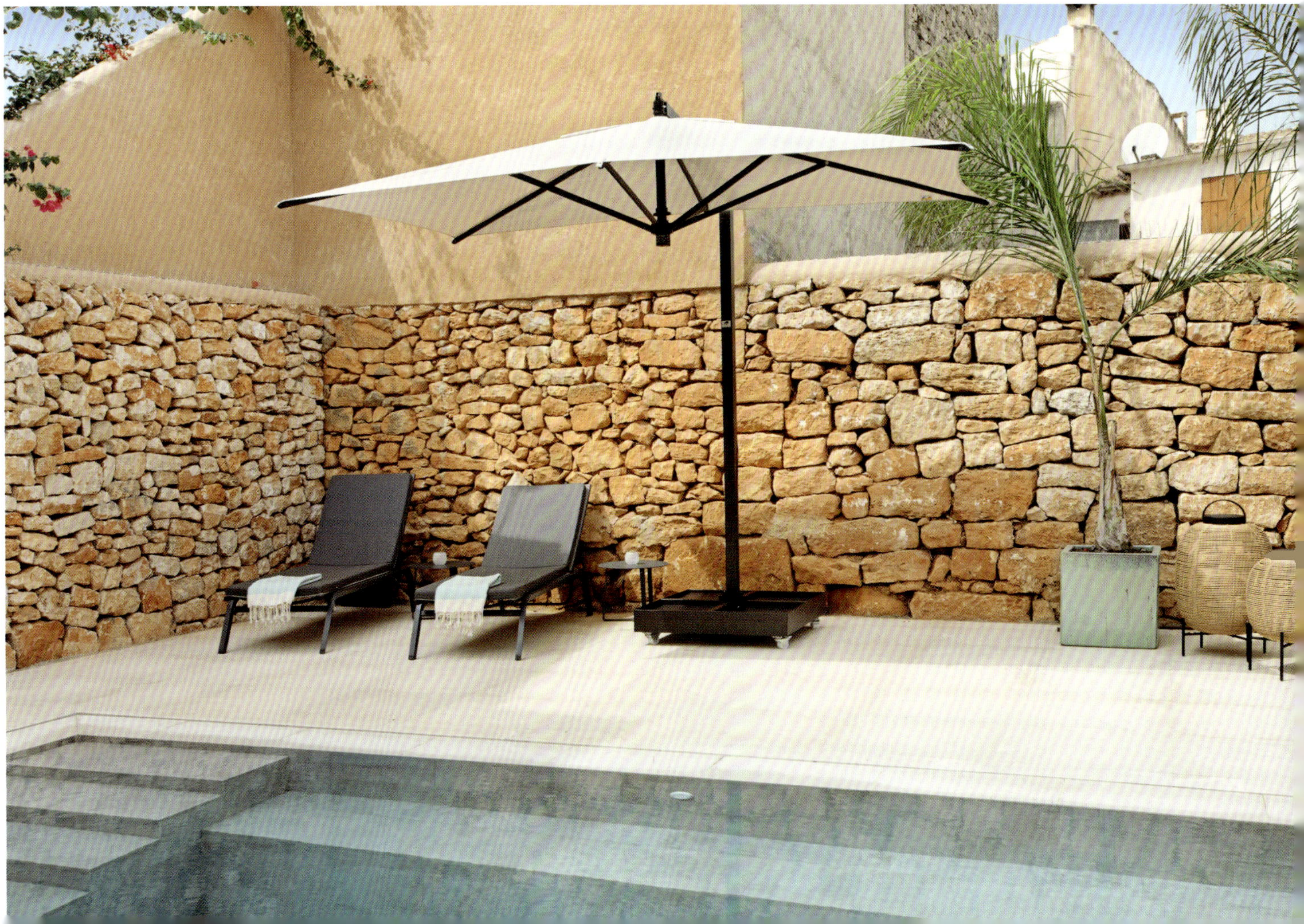

THE SELECTION OF WOODS AND THE
INCORPORATION OF THREE LEVELS
ALONG WITH A LIGHTBOX BRING THE
INTERIOR SPACES TO LIFE, FLOODING
THEM WITH A WARM LUMINOSITY

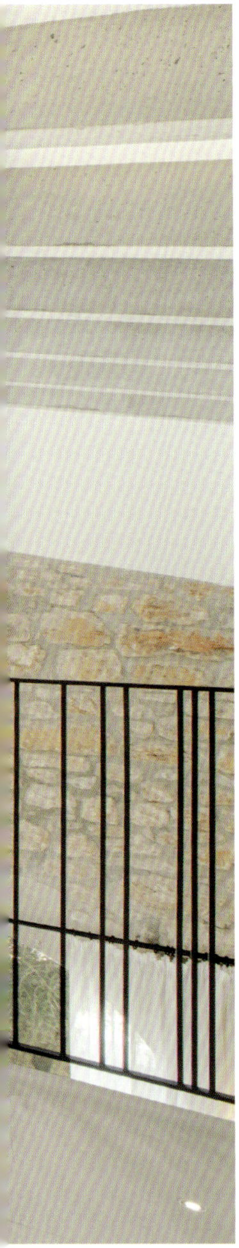

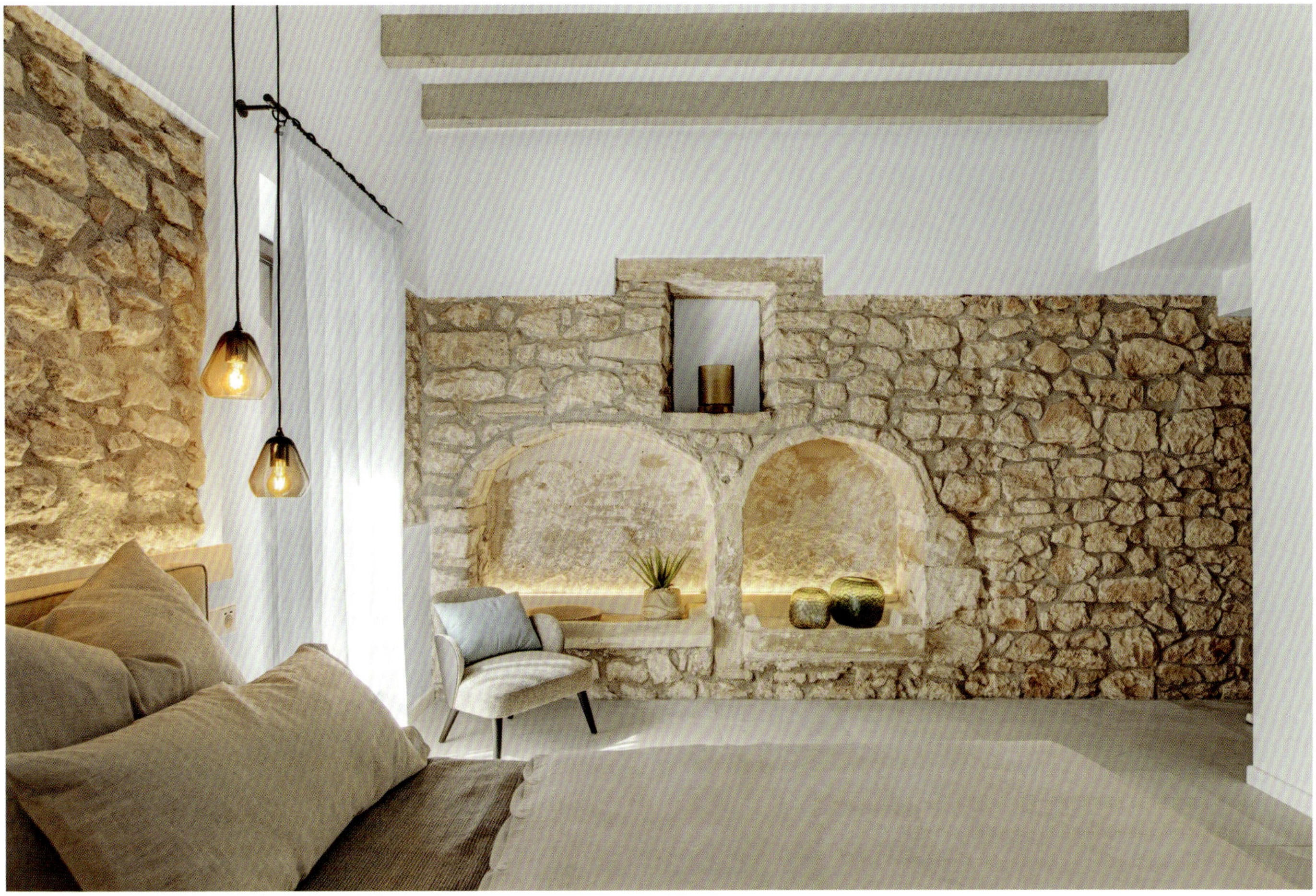

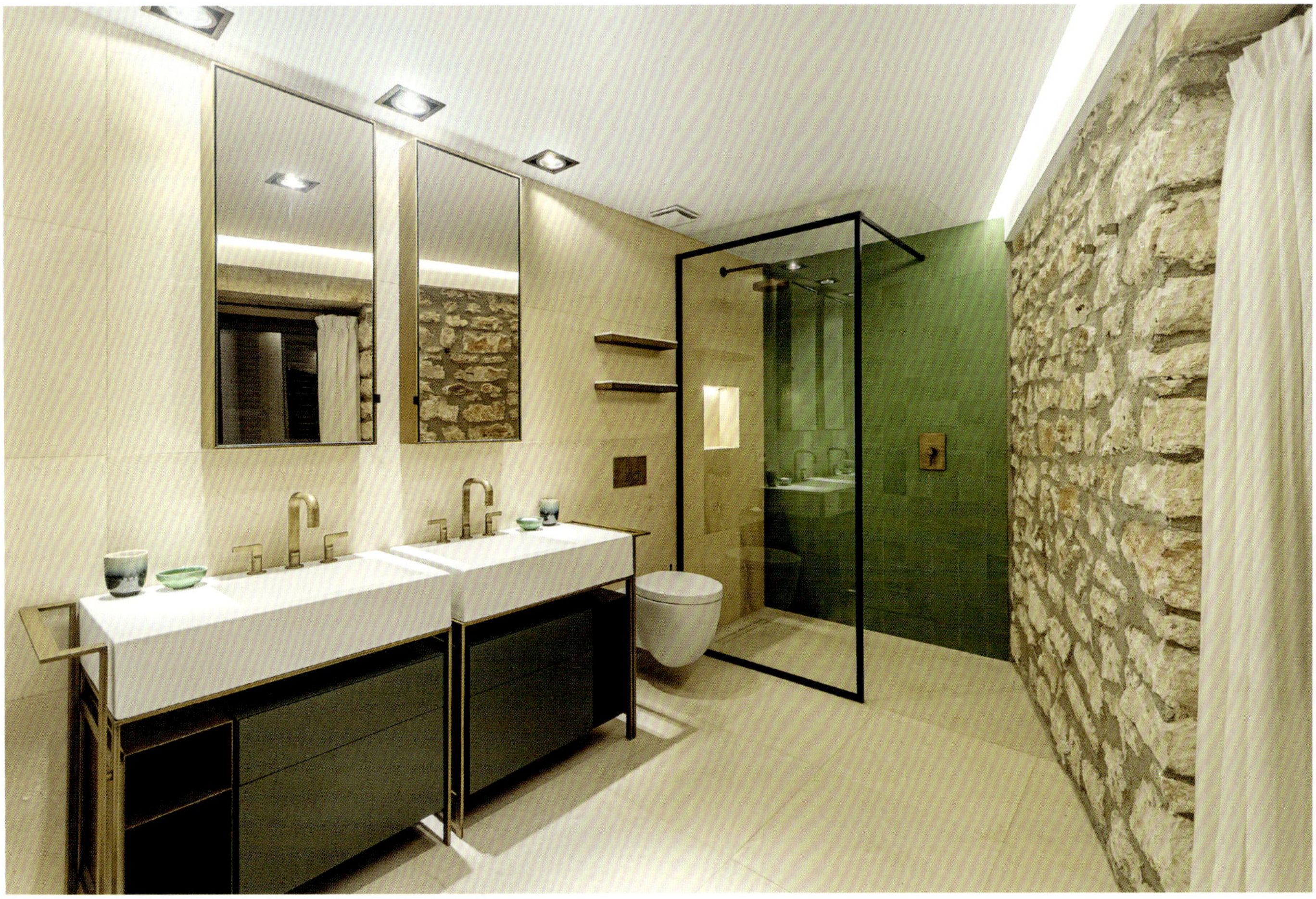

RIALTO LIVING
INTERIOR DESIGN
STUDIO

HOTEL SON BUNYOLA

BANYALBUFAR

Photos © Pär Olsson

Nestled in one of the most beautiful, wild, and secluded corners of the Tramuntana mountain range stands this stately home, whose origins trace back to the 13th century. Designed around a central courtyard, the building retains characteristic elements of Mallorcan agricultural architecture, such as the olive press and water cisterns. The architectural renovation was overseen by GRAS Reynés Arquitectos, who successfully preserved and enhanced its historical authenticity, while the landscaping by Jardins de Tramuntana harmoniously integrates with the natural surroundings. The interior design project by Rialto Living sought to preserve the eclectic and historical spirit of the property, reflecting the essence and distinctive character of the island's north coast. Inspired by the colors, textures, and patterns of Mallorca, each space has been designed with a unique identity, incorporating exclusive pieces and artworks by local artists with close ties to the island. The pool stands out, surrounded by loungers and Balinese beds, offering imposing panoramic views. The fabrics designed by Klas Kall founder of Rialto Living, evoke the island's beauty and integrate harmoniously into the interior design, creating a unique residential experience.

Eingebettet in eine der schönsten, wildesten und abgelegensten Ecken des Tramuntana-Gebirges steht dieses herrschaftliche Haus, dessen Ursprünge bis ins 13. Jahrhundert zurückreichen. Das Gebäude ist um einen zentralen Innenhof herum angelegt und enthält charakteristische Elemente der mallorquinischen Landwirtschaftsarchitektur, wie die Olivenpresse und die Wasserzisternen. Die architektonische Renovierung wurde von GRAS Reynés Arquitectos geleitet, die die historische Authentizität erfolgreich bewahrt und verbessert haben, während sich die Landschaftsgestaltung von Jardins de Tramuntana harmonisch in die natürliche Umgebung einfügt. Das Innenarchitekturprojekt von Rialto Living zielte darauf ab, den eklektischen und historischen Geist des Anwesens zu bewahren und die Essenz und den unverwechselbaren Charakter der Nordküste der Insel widerzuspiegeln. Inspiriert von den Farben, Texturen und Mustern Mallorcas, wurde jeder Raum mit einer eigenen Identität gestaltet und mit exklusiven Stücken und Kunstwerken von lokalen Künstlern, die eine enge Verbindung zur Insel haben, ausgestattet. Der Pool sticht hervor, umgeben von Liegen und balinesischen Betten, und bietet einen beeindruckenden Panoramablick. Die von Klas Kall entworfenen Stoffe erinnern an die Schönheit der Insel und fügen sich harmonisch in das Innendesign ein, so dass ein einzigartiges Wohngefühl entsteht.

Nichée dans l'un des coins les plus beaux, sauvages et reculés de la Sierra de Tramuntana, se dresse cette demeure seigneuriale dont les origines remontent au XIIIᵉ siècle. Conçu autour d'une cour centrale, le bâtiment conserve des éléments caractéristiques de l'architecture agricole mallorquine, tels que le pressoir à huile et les citernes d'eau. La rénovation architecturale a été réalisée par GRAS Reynés Arquitectos, qui ont su préserver et valoriser son authenticité historique, tandis que l'aménagement paysager conçu par Jardins de Tramuntana s'intègre harmonieusement à l'environnement naturel. Le projet de design intérieur par Rialto Living a cherché à préserver l'esprit éclectique et historique de la propriété, reflétant l'essence et le caractère distinctif de la côte nord de l'île. Inspiré par les couleurs, les textures et les motifs de Majorque, chaque espace a été conçu avec une identité unique, intégrant des pièces exclusives et des œuvres d'artistes locaux ayant des liens étroits avec l'île. La piscine se distingue, entourée de chaises longues et de lits balinais offrant des vues panoramiques impressionnantes. Les tissus conçus par Klas Kall fondateur de Rialto Living, évoquent la beauté de l'île et s'intègrent harmonieusement dans le design intérieur, créant une expérience résidentielle unique.

Enclavada en uno de los rincones más bellos, silvestres y escondidos de la sierra de Tramuntana emerge esta casa señorial cuyos orígenes se remontan al siglo XIII. A partir de un diseño estructurado en torno a un patio central, la edificación conserva elementos característicos de la arquitectura agrícola mallorquina, como la almazara y los aljibes. La renovación arquitectónica estuvo a cargo de GRAS Reynés Arquitectos, quienes han sabido preservar y realzar la autenticidad histórica, mientras que el paisajismo diseñado por Jardins de Tramuntana se integra armoniosamente con la naturaleza. El proyecto de interiorismo a cargo de Rialto Living ha buscado preservar el espíritu ecléctico e histórico de la propiedad, reflejando la esencia y el carácter distintivo de la costa norte de la isla. Inspirados en los colores, texturas y patrones de Mallorca, cada espacio ha sido diseñado con una identidad única, incorporando piezas exclusivas y obras de artistas locales con estrechos vínculos con la isla. Destaca la piscina rodeada de hamacas y camas balinesas con imponentes vistas panorámicas. Las telas, diseñadas por Klas Kall, fundador de Rialto Living, evocan la belleza de la isla y se integran armoniosamente en el interiorismo, creando una experiencia residencial única.

THE INTERIOR DESIGN AIMED TO
RETAIN THE PROPERTY'S ECLECTIC
AND HISTORICAL ESSENCE

RÔCK & VILLA

CASA MARGARITA

SANTA MARGALIDA

Photos © Salva López

Casa Margarita is a village house that combines the historic charm of the island's traditional constructions with contemporary comfort and luxury. The building, dating back to 1890, holds cultural value for the local community, which is why Rôck&Villa has rehabilitated the house, preserving its original features with special sensitivity. The 222 m² property includes a Mediterranean garden with a pool and an independent guest house. The house offers a serene and welcoming atmosphere. Neutral colors envelop every corner, while natural and warm textures add depth and warmth to the environments. The furniture was custom-designed by the builders and crafted by local artisans.

The meticulous restoration of Casa Margarita focused on preserving original architectural elements while incorporating high-quality finishes. Paulo and Stefan, experts in revitalizing historic homes, have managed to blend traditional charm with modern luxury in this property that reflects the rich history and architectural heritage of Mallorca.

Casa Margarita ist ein Dorfhaus, das den historischen Charme der traditionellen Bauweise der Insel mit modernem Komfort und Luxus vereint. Das Gebäude aus dem Jahr 1890 hat kulturellen Wert für die lokale Gemeinschaft, weshalb Rôck&Villa das Haus mit besonderer Sensibilität für seine ursprünglichen Merkmale restauriert hat.

Das 222 Quadratmeter große Anwesen umfasst einen mediterranen Garten mit Pool und ein unabhängiges Gästehaus. Das Haus bietet eine ruhige und einladende Atmosphäre. Neutrale Farben durchziehen jede Ecke, während natürliche und warme Texturen Tiefe und Wärme in die Umgebungen bringen. Die Möbel wurden von den Bauherren maßgefertigt und von lokalen Handwerkern gefertigt.

Die sorgfältige Restaurierung von Casa Margarita konzentrierte sich darauf, originale architektonische Elemente zu bewahren und gleichzeitig hochwertige Oberflächen zu integrieren. Paulo und Stefan, Experten für die Revitalisierung historischer Häuser, haben es geschafft, traditionellen Charme mit modernem Luxus in dieser Immobilie zu verbinden, die die reiche Geschichte und das architektonische Erbe Mallorcas widerspiegelt.

Casa Margarita est une maison de village qui combine le charme historique des constructions traditionnelles de l'île avec le confort et le luxe contemporains. Le bâtiment, datant de 1890, a une valeur culturelle pour la communauté locale, c'est pourquoi Rôck&Villa a réhabilité la maison en préservant ses caractéristiques originales avec une sensibilité particulière.

La propriété de 222 mètres carrés comprend un jardin méditerranéen avec piscine et une maison d'hôtes indépendante. La maison offre une atmosphère sereine et accueillante. Les couleurs neutres enveloppent chaque recoin, tandis que les textures naturelles et chaleureuses ajoutent profondeur et chaleur aux environnements. Les meubles ont été conçus sur mesure par les constructeurs et fabriqués par des artisans locaux.

La restauration méticuleuse de Casa Margarita s'est concentrée sur la préservation des éléments architecturaux originaux tout en incorporant des finitions de haute qualité. Paulo et Stefan, experts en revitalisation de maisons historiques, ont réussi à fusionner le charme traditionnel avec le luxe moderne dans cette propriété qui reflète la riche histoire et le patrimoine architectural de Majorque.

Casa Margarita es una vivienda de pueblo que combina el encanto histórico de las construcciones tradicionales de la isla, con las comodidades y el lujo contemporáneo. La edificación que data del año 1890 tiene un valor cultural para la comunidad local, por eso Rôck&Villa ha rehabilitado la casa preservando sus características originales con especial sensibilidad.

La propiedad de 222 m² incluye un jardín mediterráneo con piscina y una casa de huéspedes independiente. La vivienda ofrece una atmósfera serena y acogedora. Los colores neutros envuelven cada rincón, mientras que las texturas naturales y cálidas añaden profundidad y calidez a los ambientes. Los muebles fueron diseñados a medida por los constructores y elaborados por artesanos locales.

La meticulosa restauración de Casa Margarita se centró en preservar elementos arquitectónicos originales mientras se incorporaban acabados de alta calidad. Paulo y Stefan, expertos en revitalizar viviendas históricas, han logrado fusionar el encanto tradicional con el lujo moderno en esta propiedad, que refleja la rica historia y el patrimonio arquitectónico de Mallorca.

CASA MARGARITA'S METICULOUS
RESTORATION PRESERVED ORIGINAL
ARCHITECTURAL ELEMENTS AND ADDED
HIGH-QUALITY FINISHES

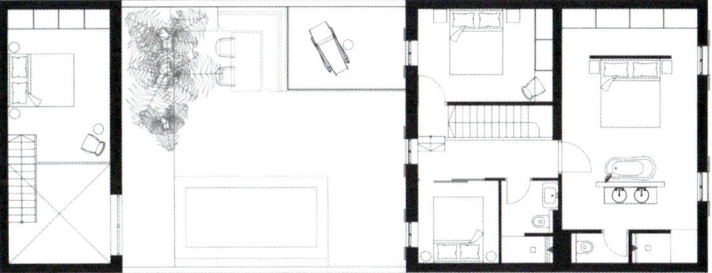

First floor plan

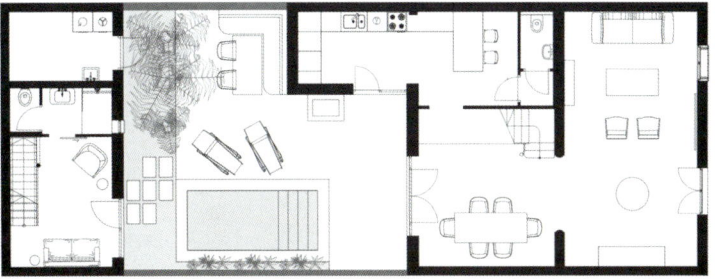

Ground floor plan

SOLÍS BETANCOURT & SHERRILL

CASA DE CAMPO

ESPORLES

Photos © Marcos Galvany

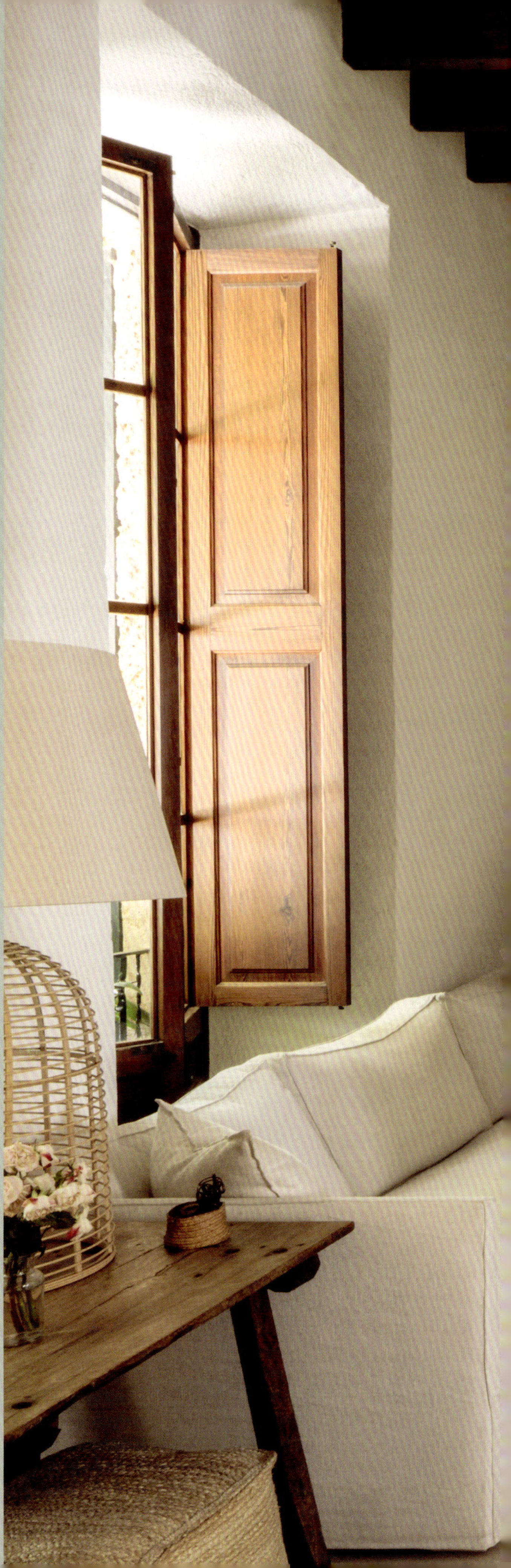

This country house, merging two contiguous buildings that were abandoned and deteriorated, is located in the picturesque town of Esporles, in the heart of the Tramuntana mountains. Interior designers José Solís Betancourt and Paul Sherrill envisioned combining the buildings to create grander open spaces while maintaining the simple, elegant, vernacular charm of the region.

During the restoration process, the characteristic stone walls and limestone pavement of traditional Mallorcan architecture were preserved. Existing stone and wooden beams were also left intact. The new additions were integrated with the original, reflecting the essence of the building.

The interior decoration follows this philosophy of mixing rustic aesthetics with contemporary ones. The color palette is natural and fresh, with shades of stone, sand, and wood creating serene and harmonious environments. Simple and functional furniture combines modern pieces with family antiques, adding character and depth to the spaces. The result is a home that respects its history and surroundings while offering comfort and design adapted to the present day.

Dieses Landhaus, das zwei benachbarte Gebäude vereint, die ungenutzt und verfallen waren, befindet sich in der malerischen Stadt Esporles im Herzen des Tramuntana-Gebirges. Die Innendesigner José Solís Betancourt und Paul Sherrill leiteten das Renovierungsprojekt, um das Anwesen in neuen Glanz zu versetzen.

Während des Restaurierungsprozesses wurden die charakteristischen Steinmauern und der Kalksteinbelag der traditionellen mallorquinischen Architektur erhalten. Auch vorhandene Steine und Holzbalken blieben intakt. Die neuen Ergänzungen wurden in das Original integriert und spiegeln die Essenz des Gebäudes wider.

Die Inneneinrichtung folgt dieser Philosophie und mischt rustikale Ästhetik mit zeitgenössischen Elementen. Die Farbpalette ist natürlich und frisch, mit Nuancen von Stein, Sand und Holz, die ruhige und harmonische Umgebungen schaffen. Einfache und funktionale Möbel kombinieren moderne Stücke mit Familienantiquitäten und verleihen den Räumen Charakter und Tiefe. Das Ergebnis ist ein Haus, das seine Geschichte und Umgebung respektiert und gleichzeitig Komfort und Design bietet, die an die heutige Zeit angepasst sind.

Cette maison de campagne, fusionnant deux bâtiments contigus qui étaient abandonné et détériorés, est située dans la pittoresque ville d'Esporles, au cœur de la Serra de Tramuntana. Les designers d'intérieur José Solís Betancourt et Paul Sherrill ont réuni les bâtiments pour créer de plus grands espaces ouverts, tout en conservant le charme simple, élégant et vernaculaire de la région.

Lors du processus de restauration, les murs en pierre caractéristiques et le pavement en calcaire de l'architecture traditionnelle majorquine ont été préservés. Les pierres et les poutres en bois existantes ont également été laissées intactes. Les nouvelles additions ont été intégrées à l'original, reflétant l'essence du bâtiment.

La décoration intérieure suit cette philosophie, mélangeant l'esthétique rustique avec des éléments contemporains. La palette de couleurs est naturelle et fraîche, avec des nuances de pierre, de sable et de bois créant des environnements sereins et harmonieux. Des meubles simples et fonctionnels combinent des pièces modernes avec des antiquités familiales, ajoutant caractère et profondeur aux espaces. Le résultat est une maison qui respecte son histoire et son environnement tout en offrant confort et design adaptés à l'époque actuelle.

Esta casa de campo que fusiona dos construcciones contiguas que estaban abandonados y deterioradas, se encuentra en la pintoresca localidad de Esporles, en plena Serra Tramuntana. Los interioristas José Solís Betancourt y Paul Sherrill unieron los edificios para crear espacios abiertos más amplios, manteniendo el encanto sencillo, elegante y vernáculo de la región.

En el proceso de restauración se preservaron los muros de piedra y el pavimento de caliza, característicos de la arquitectura mallorquina tradicional. También se dejó la piedra existente y las vigas de madera. Las nuevas adiciones se integraron con lo original, reflejando la esencia de la edificación.

La decoración interior sigue esta filosofía, mezclando la estética rústica con la contemporánea. La paleta cromática es natural y fresca, con tonalidades de piedra, arena y madera, creando ambientes serenos y armoniosos. Los muebles, de estilo sencillo y funcional, combinan piezas modernas con antigüedades familiares, aportando carácter y profundidad a los espacios. El resultado es una vivienda que respeta su historia y entorno, ofreciendo un confort y diseño adaptado a la época actual.

THE COLOR PALETTE IS NATURAL AND FRESH, WITH
SHADES OF STONE, SAND AND WOOD, CREATING SERENE
AND HARMONIOUS ENVIRONMENTS

TARRAGONA-HÖHNE ARQUITECTOS + JORGE BIBILONI STUDIO

CBF HOUSE

PORTALS NOUS

Photos © Tomeu Canyelles

Designed to maximize natural light entry and offer panoramic views, this two-level residence stands out for its good integration of contemporary design into the natural environment. The façade alternates natural stone with smooth white surfaces. Mediterranean plants and shrubs in the front garden and wood on the porch ceiling introduce warmth in contrast to the minimalist architecture proposed by the Tarragona Höhne studio.

Complementing the architecture, the interior design by Jorge Bibiloni Studio provides cozy and refined environments. The interior design is organized into several functional zones with a spacious living room, a modern kitchen and bedrooms. The residence is conceived around three patios, each with an olive tree. The patio leading to the chill-out area and garden with a pool is the heart of outdoor social life and directly connects the interior with the exterior. The pool clad in green gresite adds a touch of luxury. Surrounding it are sun loungers and a paved area that integrates with the garden. The interior maintains a consistent aesthetic with micro-cement floors and lime-painted walls, reinforcing the sense of spaciousness and luminosity.

Entworfen, um das natürliche Licht zu maximieren und Panoramablicke zu bieten, zeichnet sich diese zweistöckige Residenz durch ihre gute Integration von modernem Design in die natürliche Umgebung aus. Die Fassade wechselt zwischen Naturstein und glatten weißen Oberflächen. Mediterrane Pflanzen und Sträucher im Vorgarten und Holz an der Decke der Veranda bringen Wärme im Kontrast zur minimalistischen Architektur, die das Studio Tarragona Höhne vorschlägt.

Ergänzend zur Architektur bietet das Innendesign von Jorge Bibiloni Studio gemütliche und raffinierte Umgebungen. Das Innendesign ist in mehrere funktionale Bereiche organisiert, mit einem geräumigen Wohnzimmer, einer modernen Küche und Schlafzimmern. Die Residenz ist um drei Patios herum konzipiert, jeder mit einem Olivenbaum. Der Patio, der zum Chill-Out-Bereich und Garten mit Pool führt, ist das Herzstück des sozialen Lebens im Freien und verbindet das Innere direkt mit dem Äußeren. Der mit grünem Gresit verkleidete Pool verleiht eine luxuriöse Note. Er ist umgeben von Liegestühlen und einer gepflasterten Fläche, die sich in den Garten integriert. Das Innere behält eine konsistente Ästhetik mit Mikrozementböden und kalkfarbenen Wänden bei, was das Gefühl von Geräumigkeit und Helligkeit verstärkt.

Entworfen, um das natürliche Licht zu maximieren und Panoramablicke zu bieten, zeichnet sich diese zweistöckige Residenz durch ihre gute Integration von modernem Design in die natürliche Umgebung aus. Die Fassade wechselt zwischen Naturstein und glatten weißen Oberflächen. Mediterrane Pflanzen und Sträucher im Vorgarten und Holz an der Decke der Veranda bringen Wärme im Kontrast zur minimalistischen Architektur, die das Studio Tarragona Höhne vorschlägt.

Ergänzend zur Architektur bietet das Innendesign von Jorge Bibiloni Studio gemütliche und raffinierte Umgebungen. Das Innendesign ist in mehrere funktionale Bereiche organisiert, mit einem geräumigen Wohnzimmer, einer modernen Küche und Schlafzimmern. Die Residenz ist um drei Patios herum konzipiert, jeder mit einem Olivenbaum. Der Patio, der zum Chill-Out-Bereich und Garten mit Pool führt, ist das Herzstück des sozialen Lebens im Freien und verbindet das Innere direkt mit dem Äußeren. Der mit grünem Gresit verkleidete Pool verleiht eine luxuriöse Note. Er ist umgeben von Liegestühlen und einer gepflasterten Fläche, die sich in den Garten integriert. Das Innere behält eine konsistente Ästhetik mit Mikrozementböden und kalkfarbenen Wänden bei, was das Gefühl von Geräumigkeit und Helligkeit verstärkt.

Diseñada para maximizar la entrada de luz natural y ofrecer vistas panorámicas, esta residencia de dos niveles destaca por la buena integración del diseño contemporáneo al entorno natural. La fachada alterna la piedra natural con superficies blancas y lisas. Las plantas y arbustos mediterráneos del jardín frontal, y la madera en el techo del porche introducen calidez en contraste con la arquitectura minimalista planteada por el estudio Tarragona Höhne.

Complementando la arquitectura, el interiorismo de Jorge Bibiloni Studio aporta ambientes acogedores y refinados. El diseño interior se organiza en varias zonas funcionales, con una amplia sala de estar, una moderna cocina y los dormitorios. La residencia está concebida alrededor de tres patios cada uno con un olivo. El patio que da a la zona de chill out y al jardín con piscina, es el corazón de la vida social al aire libre y está vinculado directamente el interior con el exterior. La piscina revestida con gresite verde aporta un toque de lujo. Le rodean las tumbonas y un área pavimentada que se integra con el jardín. El interior mantiene una estética coherente, con suelo de microcemento y paredes pintadas a la cal, reforzando la sensación de amplitud y luminosidad.

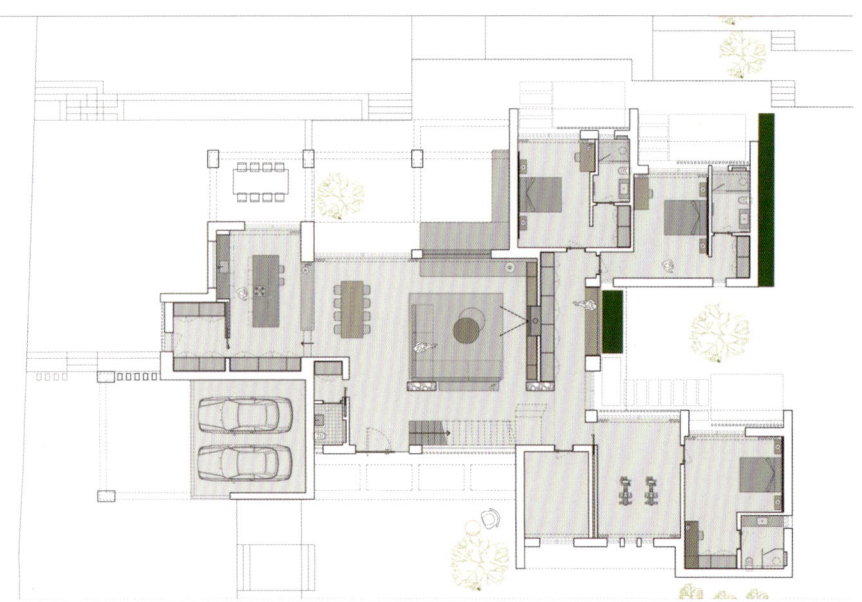

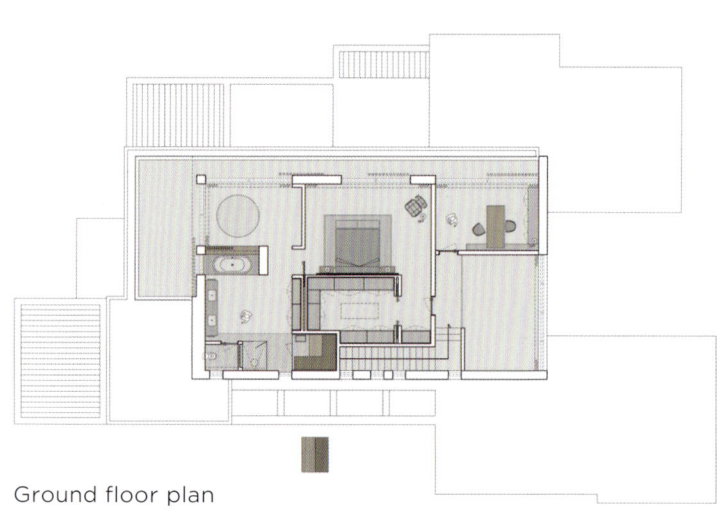

Ground floor plan

Ground floor plan

THE RESIDENCE IS CONCEIVED AROUND THREE
PATIOS, EACH WITH AN OLIVE TREE

THE EAZEY

CASA PASSARATX

PORRERES

Photos © Laia Cocoi

This house has been renovated to preserve the essence of old Mallorcan stone houses while adding a touch of Berber aesthetics through colors and textures. For the interior, a predominantly white color scheme was chosen to highlight the Mediterranean-style furniture. The floor, wall, kitchen, and bathroom coverings were hand-applied with a spatula and painted white with a hardening paint that forms an easy-to-clean surface.

Despite the clients' insistence, the designers did not want to expose the old stone walls for fear it would be associated with a resource heavily used in the 1990s. However, when the covering did not adhere, they had to expose the original stone wall and were delighted with the result for its authenticity. Both the wooden windows and shutters and the industrial doors were created by local carpenters and artisans. The patio, originally filled with large stones, was transformed into three stepped terraces, one of which houses a pool. The incomplete Mallorcan sandstone walls were restored with old stones and plastered joints.

Dieses Haus wurde renoviert, um die Essenz der alten mallorquinischen Steinhäuser zu bewahren und gleichzeitig durch Farben und Texturen einen Hauch von Berber-Ästhetik hinzuzufügen. Für das Innere wurde eine überwiegend weiße Farbgebung gewählt, um die Möbel im mediterranen Stil hervorzuheben. Die Boden-, Wand-, Küchen- und Badezimmerbeläge wurden mit einer Spachtel aufgetragen und weiß gestrichen, mit einer härtenden Farbe, die eine leicht zu reinigende Oberfläche bildet.

Trotz der Insistenz der Kunden wollten die Designer die alten Steinmauern nicht freilegen, aus Angst, dass sie mit einer in den 90er Jahren stark genutzten Ressource assoziiert würden. Als die Beschichtung jedoch nicht haftete, mussten sie die ursprüngliche Steinmauer freilegen und waren begeistert von dem Ergebnis wegen seiner Authentizität. Sowohl die Holzfenster und -läden als auch die Industrietüren wurden von lokalen Tischlern und Handwerkern gefertigt. Der ursprünglich mit großen Steinen gefüllte Innenhof wurde in drei gestufte Terrassen umgewandelt, von denen eine einen Pool beherbergt. Die unvollständigen mallorquinischen Sandsteinmauern wurden mit alten Steinen und verputzten Fugen restauriert.

Cette maison a été rénovée pour préserver l'essence des anciennes maisons en pierre majorquines tout en ajoutant une touche d'esthétique berbère à travers les couleurs et les textures. Pour l'intérieur, une gamme de couleurs principalement blanche a été choisie pour mettre en valeur le mobilier de style méditerranéen. Les revêtements de sol, murs, cuisine et salles de bains ont été appliqués à la main avec une spatule et peints en blanc avec une peinture durcissante qui forme une surface facile à nettoyer.

Malgré l'insistance des clients, les designers ne voulaient pas exposer les anciens murs en pierre par crainte qu'ils ne soient associés à une ressource largement utilisée dans les années 90. Cependant, lorsque le revêtement ne s'adhérait pas, ils ont dû exposer le mur en pierre original et ont été ravis du résultat pour son authenticité. Les fenêtres en bois, les volets et les portes industrielles ont été créés par des menuisiers et artisans locaux. Le patio, à l'origine rempli de grosses pierres, a été transformé en trois terrasses en gradins, dont une abrite une piscine. Les murs incomplets en grès majorquin ont été restaurés avec des pierres anciennes et des joints enduits.

Esta vivienda ha sido renovada para conservar la esencia de las antiguas casas de piedra mallorquinas, pero añadiendo una pátina de la estética *bereber*, a través de los colores y las texturas. Para el interior, se eligió una gama de tonos predominantemente neutros de manera que destaque el mobiliario de estilo mediterráneo. Los revestimientos de suelos, paredes, cocina y baños se hicieron a mano con una espátula y se pintaron de blanco con una pintura que endurece y forma una superficie fácil de limpiar.

Pese a la insistencia de los clientes, los diseñadores no querían exponer las paredes de piedra antiguas, por temor a que se asocie a un recurso muy utilizado en los años 90. Sin embargo, cuando el revestimiento no se adhería, tuvieron que dejar al descubierto la pared de piedra original, y quedaron encantados con el resultado por su autenticidad. Tanto las ventanas de madera, como las persianas y las puertas industriales fueron creadas por carpinteros y artesanos locales. El patio, que originalmente estaba lleno de grandes piedras, se transformó en tres terrazas escalonadas una de las cuales aloja una piscina. Las antiguas paredes de arenisca mallorquina que estaban incompletas se restauraron con piedras antiguas y juntas enlucidas.

THIS HOME HAS BEEN RENOVATED TO PRESERVE
THE ESSENCEOF OLD MALLORCAN STONE HOUSES

TNW DESIGN

CASA DEL SINDICATO

ARTÀ

Photos © Janne Peters

At least 150 years old, this three-story house has been renovated to fuse past and present. Located in the historic center of Artá, the building had been vacant and in poor condition for many years. Some parts had deteriorated and were completely rebuilt from scratch. The work lasted two years and included the supervision of an archaeologist with several excavations.

The designer Thomas Niederste-Werbeck aimed to transform this historical gem into a warm and contemporary home. To do so, he updated all installations and transformed the patio into an urban oasis with trees, a pool, and a fountain.

On the floor, the Gris Zarci stone connects the interior with the exterior, maintaining the original layout on the ground floor, although the kitchen was completely rebuilt. On the first floor, a porch overlooks the interior patio with a daybed and a curtain for privacy. The original staircase with its railings was preserved. The owners, passionate about art, have integrated references to Morocco in the decoration. All the furniture is sober and elegant in neutral tones, with a wabi-sabi style.

Mindestens 150 Jahre alt, wurde dieses dreistöckige Haus renoviert, um Vergangenheit und Gegenwart zu verschmelzen. Im historischen Zentrum von Artá gelegen, war das Gebäude viele Jahre lang unbewohnt und in schlechtem Zustand. Einige Teile waren verfallen und wurden komplett von Grund auf neu aufgebaut. Die Arbeiten dauerten zwei Jahre und umfassten die Aufsicht eines Archäologen mit mehreren Ausgrabungen.

Der Designer Thomas Niederste-Werbeck wollte dieses historische Juwel in ein warmes und zeitgemäßes Zuhause verwandeln. Dazu aktualisierte er alle Installationen und verwandelte den Innenhof in eine städtische Oase mit Bäumen, einem Pool und einem Brunnen.

Auf dem Boden verbindet der Gris Zarci-Stein das Innere mit dem Äußeren, wobei die ursprüngliche Verteilung im Erdgeschoss beibehalten wurde, obwohl die Küche komplett neu gebaut wurde. Im ersten Stock überblickt eine Veranda den Innenhof mit einem Tagesbett und einem Vorhang für Privatsphäre. Die ursprüngliche Treppe mit ihrem Geländer wurde erhalten. Die Besitzer, Kunstliebhaber, haben marokkanische Einflüsse in die Dekoration integriert. Alle Möbel sind schlicht und elegant in neutralen Tönen, mit einem wabi-sabi-Stil.

Vieille d'au moins 150 ans, cette maison de trois étages a été rénovée pour fusionner passé et présent. Située dans le centre historique d'Artá, le bâtiment avait été vacant et en mauvais état pendant de nombreuses années. Certaines parties s'étaient détériorées et ont été complètement reconstruites à partir de zéro. Les travaux ont duré deux ans et ont inclus la supervision d'un archéologue avec plusieurs fouilles.

Le designer Thomas Niederste-Werbeck a cherché à transformer ce joyau historique en une maison chaleureuse et contemporaine. Pour ce faire, il a mis à jour toutes les installations et transformé le patio en un oasis urbain avec des arbres, une piscine et une fontaine.

Au sol, la pierre Gris Zarci relie l'intérieur à l'extérieur, en maintenant la distribution originale au rez-de-chaussée, bien que la cuisine ait été entièrement reconstruite. Au premier étage, un porche donne sur le patio intérieur avec un lit de jour et un rideau pour plus d'intimité. L'escalier original avec ses balustrades a été conservé. Les propriétaires, passionnés d'art, ont intégré des références au Maroc dans la décoration. Tous les meubles sont sobres et élégants dans des tons neutres, avec un style wabi-sabi.

Con al menos 150 años de antigüedad, esta casa de tres plantas ha sido reformada para fusionar pasado y presente. Situada en el centro histórico de Artá, la construcción estuvo vacía y en mal estado durante muchos años. Algunas partes se habían deteriorado y se reconstruyeron completamente desde cero. Los trabajos duraron dos años, y contaron con la supervisión de un arqueólogo con varias excavaciones incluidas.

El diseñador Thomas Niederste-Werbeck se propuso transformar esta joya histórica en un hogar cálido y contemporáneo. Para ellos actualizó todas las instalaciones y transformó el patio en un oasis urbano con árboles, piscina y fuente.

En el suelo, la piedra Gris Zarci conecta el interior con el exterior, manteniendo la distribución original en la planta baja, aunque la cocina se reconstruyó por completo. En la primera planta un porche da al patio interior con una cama de día y una cortina que aporta privacidad. Se preservó la escalera original con sus barandillas. Los propietarios, apasionados del arte, han integrado referencias a Marruecos en la decoración. Todo el mobiliario es sobrio y elegante, en tonos neutros de estilo *wabi sabi*.

ALL THE FURNITURE IS SOBER AND ELEGANT IN
NEUTRAL TONES, WITH A WABI-SABI STYLE

P. 6

FS HOME

3 5 3   A R Q U I T E C T E S

A N T Ò N I A   P I Z À

CONSTRUCTOR: TOMEU PIZÁ,
CONSTRUCCIONES SES PLANES D'ALARÓ

MALLORCA, SPAIN
353ARQUITECTES.COM

353 Arquitectes is a team of professionals in architecture, interior design, and urban planning led by architect Antònia Pizà. With over 20 years of experience, the firm undertakes projects ranging from rustic to contemporary settings, always in dialogue with the environment. Their works aim to integrate architecture into the environment with minimal impact, improving the existing footprint. The firm maintains rigorous technical control of materials and costs throughout the construction process, provides environmental improvement advice and energy resource use, and manages administrative procedures for project development, ensuring efficient execution in compliance with regulations.

353 Arquitectes ist ein Team von Fachleuten in Architektur, Innendesign und Stadtplanung, das von der Architektin Antònia Pizà geleitet wird. Mit über 20 Jahren Erfahrung realisiert das Unternehmen Projekte von rustikalen bis hin zu zeitgenössischen Umgebungen, immer im Dialog mit der Umwelt. Ihre Arbeiten zielen darauf ab, die Architektur mit minimalem Einfluss in die Umgebung zu integrieren und den bestehenden Fußabdruck zu verbessern. Das Unternehmen hält eine strenge technische Kontrolle der Materialien und Kosten während des gesamten Bauprozesses aufrecht, bietet Beratung zur Umweltverbesserung und Nutzung von Energiequellen und verwaltet die administrativen Verfahren für die Entwicklung jedes Projekts und stellt eine effiziente Umsetzung in Übereinstimmung mit den Vorschriften sicher.

353 Arquitectes est une équipe de professionnels en architecture, design d'intérieur et urbanisme dirigée par l'architecte Antònia Pizà. Avec plus de 20 ans d'expérience, l'entreprise réalise des projets allant des environnements rustiques aux contemporains, toujours en dialogue avec l'environnement. Leurs travaux visent à intégrer l'architecture dans l'environnement avec un impact minimal, améliorant l'empreinte existante. L'entreprise maintient un contrôle technique rigoureux des matériaux et des coûts tout au long du processus de construction, offre des conseils sur l'amélioration environnementale et l'utilisation des ressources énergétiques, et gère les procédures administratives pour le développement de chaque projet, assurant une exécution efficace en conformité avec les normes.

353 Arquitectes es un equipo de profesionales en arquitectura, interiorismo y urbanismo, dirigido por la arquitecta Antònia Pizà. Con más de 20 años de trayectoria, la firma realiza proyectos que abarcan desde ámbitos rústicos hasta entornos contemporáneos, siempre en diálogo con el entorno. Sus trabajos están orientados a integrar la arquitectura en el entorno con el mínimo impacto, mejorando la huella existente. La firma mantiene un riguroso control técnico de materiales y costes durante todo el proceso constructivo, realiza asesoramiento de mejora medioambiental y del uso de recursos energéticos. Además, gestionan los trámites administrativos para el desarrollo de cada proyecto, asegurando una ejecución eficiente y conforme a la normativa.

SAT CHIT ANANDA

BCONNECTED
REAL ESTATE,
ARCHITECTURE &
INTERIOR DESIGN

CHRISTINE LEJA
ANDREE MIENKUS

MALLORCA, SPAIN
BCONNECTEDMALLORCA.COM

Founded in Mallorca in the late 1990s by Christine Leja and Andree Mienkus, bconnected Real Estate, Architecture & Interior Design is an internationally recognized full circle company. The firm stands out for its unique designs resulting from a balanced and surprising combination of textures, colors, volumes, and styles. Properties designed by bconnected have become collectible pieces. Their works tell stories through a colorful, inspired, bold, energetic, and empathetic approach. When asked how they constantly reinvent themselves, Christine Leja likes to quote Mark Twain: "Whenever you find yourself on the side of the majority, it is time to pause and reflect."

Gegründet auf Mallorca in den späten 1990er Jahren von Christine Leja und Andree Mienkus, ist bconnected Real Estate, Architektur & Interior Design ein international anerkanntes Unternehmen, das alle Bereiche abdeckt. Das Unternehmen zeichnet sich durch einzigartige Designs aus, die aus einer ausgewogenen und überraschenden Kombination von Texturen, Farben, Volumen und Stilen resultieren. Von bconnected entworfene Immobilien sind zu Sammlerstücken geworden. Ihre Werke erzählen Geschichten durch einen farbenfrohen, inspirierten, mutigen, energetischen und einfühlsamen Ansatz. Auf die Frage, wie sie sich ständig neu erfinden, zitiert Christine Leja gerne Mark Twain: „Wann immer du dich auf der Seite der Mehrheit befindest, ist es Zeit, innezuhalten und nachzudenken."

Fondée à Majorque à la fin des années 1990 par Christine Leja et Andree Mienkus, bconnected Real Estate, Architecture & Interior Design est un une entreprise intégrale de renommée internationale. L'entreprise se distingue par des designs uniques résultant d'une combinaison équilibrée et surprenante de textures, de couleurs, de volumes et de styles. Les propriétés conçues par bconnected sont devenues des pièces de collection. Leurs œuvres racontent des histoires à travers une approche colorée, inspirée, audacieuse, énergique et empathique. Lorsqu'on lui demande comment ils se réinventent constamment, Christine Leja aime citer Mark Twain : « Chaque fois que vous vous trouvez du côté de la majorité, il est temps de s'arrêter et de réfléchir ».

Fundado en Mallorca a finales de la década de 1990 por Christine Leja y Andree Mienkus, bconnected Real Estate, Architecture & Interior Design, es una empresa integral de reconocimiento internacional. La firma se distingue por unos diseños únicos resultado de una combinación equilibrada y sorprendente de texturas, colores, volúmenes y estilos. Las propiedades diseñadas por bconnected se han convertido en piezas de colección. Sus trabajos cuentan historias a través de un enfoque colorido, inspirado, valiente, enérgico y empático. A la pregunta de cómo logran reinventarse constantemente, a Christine Leja le gusta citar la frase de Mark Twain: «Siempre que te encuentres del lado de lo que hace todo el mundo, es hora de reformar».

P. 28

HOTEL BAREFOOT

CARLOS SERRA
INTERIORISMO

CARLOS SERRA

VALENCIA, SPAIN
CARLOSSERRAINTERIORISMO.COM

Carlos Serra (1968) is an interior designer with over 25 years of experience in Valencia, Alicante, Castellón, Mallorca, and Madrid. Following his success with Hotel Ferrero, he has specialized in designing luxury establishments such as hotels, restaurants, and commercial premises.
The Valencian designer stands out for his ability to create modern and functional yet warm and sober environments, a balance that has become his hallmark. Recognitions such as those awarded by Condé Nast's Traveller magazine endorse his distinctive approach and constant pursuit of customer satisfaction.

Carlos Serra (1968) ist ein Innenarchitekt mit über 25 Jahren Erfahrung in Valencia, Alicante, Castellón, Mallorca und Madrid. Nach seinem Erfolg mit dem Hotel Ferrero spezialisierte er sich auf die Gestaltung von Luxus-Einrichtungen wie Hotels, Restaurants und Geschäftsräumen.
Der valencianische Designer zeichnet sich durch seine Fähigkeit aus, moderne und funktionale, aber dennoch warme und nüchterne Umgebungen zu schaffen, ein Gleichgewicht, das zu seinem Markenzeichen geworden ist. Anerkennungen wie die des Condé Nast Traveller Magazins bestätigen seinen unverwechselbaren Ansatz und seine ständige Suche nach Kundenzufriedenheit.

Carlos Serra (1968) est un designer d'intérieur avec plus de 25 ans d'expérience à Valence, Alicante, Castellón, Majorque et Madrid. Suite à son succès avec l'hôtel Ferrero, il s'est spécialisé dans la conception d'établissements de luxe tels que des hôtels, des restaurants et des locaux commerciaux.
Le designer valencien se distingue par sa capacité à créer des environnements modernes et fonctionnels, tout en étant chaleureux et sobres, un équilibre devenu sa marque de fabrique. Des distinctions comme celles décernées par le magazine Traveller de Condé Nast avalisent son approche distinctive et sa recherche constante de la satisfaction du client.

Carlos Serra (1968) es un diseñador de interiores con más de 25 años de experiencia en Valencia, Alicante, Castellón, Mallorca y Madrid. Tras su éxito en el hotel Ferrero, se ha especializado en el diseño de establecimientos de lujo, como hoteles, restaurantes y locales comerciales.
El diseñador valenciano destaca por su habilidad para crear ambientes modernos y funcionales, a la vez cálidos y sobrios, un equilibrio que se ha convertido en su seña de identidad. Reconocimientos como los otorgados por la revista Traveller de Condé Nast avalan su enfoque distintivo y su constante búsqueda de la satisfacción del cliente.

SOL DE MALLORCA

C M V   A R C H I T E C T S

A N D R E U   C R E S P Í
P E P   V I C H
H E L E N A   M O N T E S
T O L O   C U R S A C H
L L U I S   E S C A R M Í S
R U B É N   B E R M Ú D E Z

MALLORCA, BARCELONA, LANZAROTE,
HO CHI MINH
CMV-ARCHITECTS.COM

CMV Architects is an internationally award-winning architecture firm. Founded in 1996 in Palma de Mallorca (Spain), CMV has expanded internationally with offices in Spain and Vietnam. Specializing in contemporary architecture, interior design, and urbanism, their focus is on cultural, social, and urban integration, ensuring the functionality of each design. From conception to execution, CMV Architects strives to blend creativity with technical excellence, offering innovative and sustainable solutions.

CMV Architects ist ein international preisgekröntes Architekturbüro. Gegründet 1996 in Palma de Mallorca (Spanien), hat sich CMV international mit Büros in Spanien und Vietnam erweitert. Spezialisiert auf zeitgenössische Architektur, Innendesign und Städtebau konzentrieren sie sich auf kulturelle, soziale und städtische Integration und gewährleisten die Funktionalität jedes Designs. Von der Konzeption bis zur Ausführung strebt CMV Architects danach, Kreativität mit technischer Exzellenz zu verbinden und innovative und nachhaltige Lösungen anzubieten.

CMV Architects est une entreprise d'architecture primée internationalement. Fondée en 1996 à Palma de Majorque (Espagne), CMV s'est étendue à l'international avec des bureaux en Espagne et au Vietnam. Spécialisée dans des projets contemporains d'architecture, design d'intérieur et urbanisme, leur approche se concentre sur l'intégration culturelle, sociale et urbanistique, garantissant la fonctionnalité de chaque design. De la conception à l'exécution, CMV Architects s'efforce de fusionner créativité et excellence technique, offrant des solutions innovantes et durables.

CMV Architects es una firma de arquitectura galardonada internacionalmente. Fundada en 1996 en Palma de Mallorca (España), CMV se ha expandido internacionalmente, con oficinas en España y Vietnam. Especializada en proyectos contemporáneos de arquitectura, interiorismo y urbanismo, su enfoque se centra en la integración cultural, social y urbanística, garantizando la funcionalidad de cada diseño. Desde la concepción hasta la ejecución, CMV Architects se esfuerza por fusionar la creatividad con la excelencia técnica, ofreciendo soluciones innovadoras y sostenibles.

P. 46

BN1 HOUSE

DOMUM PROJECTS

JORGE BIBILONI
PEP TORRES
FERNANDO GARCÍA

MALLORCA, SPAIN
DOMUMPROJECTS.COM

Located in the heart of Palma de Mallorca, DOMUM PROJECTS specializes in architecture and interior design. Their team, composed of architects, designers, and project managers, ensures the success of any project. The firm manages both residential and commercial projects, whether new constructions or renovations, covering all phases from locating the right plot to handing over the keys. Their style is defined by warm minimalism and a Mediterranean aesthetic, avoiding excessive decorative elements to achieve elegant and timeless spaces. They use natural materials such as stone and wood, the fundamental basis of all their projects, creating harmonious and sophisticated environments.

Im Herzen von Palma de Mallorca gelegen, spezialisiert sich DOMUM PROJECTS auf Architektur und Innendesign. Ihr Team, bestehend aus Architekten, Designern und Projektmanagern, gewährleistet den Erfolg jedes Projekts. Das Unternehmen verwaltet Wohn- und Gewerbeprojekte, sei es Neubauten oder Renovierungen, und deckt alle Phasen ab, von der Standortsuche bis zur Schlüsselübergabe. Ihr Stil ist definiert durch warmen Minimalismus und eine mediterrane Ästhetik, die übermäßige dekorative Elemente vermeidet, um elegante und zeitlose Räume zu schaffen. Sie verwenden natürliche Materialien wie Stein und Holz, die die Grundlage aller ihrer Projekte bilden und harmonische und raffinierte Umgebungen schaffen.

Située au cœur de Palma de Majorque, DOMUM PROJECTS se spécialise en architecture et design d'intérieur. Leur équipe, composée d'architectes, de designers et de chefs de projet, assure le succès de tout projet. L'entreprise gère des projets résidentiels et commerciaux, qu'il s'agisse de nouvelles constructions ou de rénovations, couvrant toutes les phases, de la localisation du terrain approprié à la remise des clés. Leur style se définit par un minimalisme chaleureux et une esthétique méditerranéenne, évitant l'excès d'éléments décoratifs pour créer des espaces élégants et intemporels. Ils utilisent des matériaux naturels tels que la pierre et le bois, base fondamentale de tous leurs projets, créant des environnements harmonieux et sophistiqués.

DOMUM PROJECTS, situado en el corazón de Palma de Mallorca, se especializa en arquitectura y diseño de interiores. Su equipo, compuesto por arquitectos, diseñadores y project managers, asegura el éxito de cualquier proyecto. La firma gestiona tanto proyectos residenciales como comerciales, ya sean de obra nueva o reforma, abarcando todas las fases: desde la localización del terreno adecuado hasta la entrega de llaves. Su estilo se define por un minimalismo cálido y una estética mediterránea, evitando el exceso de elementos decorativos para lograr espacios elegantes y atemporales. Emplean materiales naturales como piedra y madera, base fundamental en todos sus proyectos, creando ambientes armoniosos y sofisticados.

CASA ORIENT   CALA EGOS

GINARD
LUETHJE WOLF –
ARCHITECTS &
DESIGNERS

SEBASTIÀ GINARD ADROVER
LARS LÜTHJE
NINA WOLF

MALLORCA, SPAIN
GLW-ARCHITECTS.COM

Based in Palma and Portopetro, Ginard Luethje Wolf is a German-Mallorcan creative team specializing in architecture and interior design. Their approach is distinguished by visually clear and harmonious aesthetics without excessive ornamentation. With extensive local experience, the team ensures the connection between the concept and the execution of each project, from new developments to complete renovations. The team consists of Sebastià Ginard Adrover, an architect with international experience; Lars Lüthje, an expert in interior design and lighting; and Nina Wolf, a designer specializing in color. Together, they offer a multidisciplinary approach to creating exceptional spaces that reflect the beauty and functionality of Mediterranean and timeless style.

Mit Sitz in Palma und Portopetro ist Ginard Luethje Wolf ein deutsch-mallorquinisches Kreativteam, das sich auf Architektur und Innendesign spezialisiert hat. Ihr Ansatz zeichnet sich durch eine visuell klare und harmonische Ästhetik ohne übermäßige Ornamentik aus. Mit umfangreicher lokaler Erfahrung sorgt das Team dafür, dass das Konzept und die Umsetzung jedes Projekts miteinander verbunden sind, von neuen Entwicklungen bis hin zu umfassenden Renovierungen. Das Team besteht aus Sebastià Ginard Adrover, einem Architekten mit internationaler Erfahrung; Lars Lüthje, Experte für Innendesign und Beleuchtung; und Nina Wolf, Designerin spezialisiert auf Farbe. Gemeinsam bieten sie einen multidisziplinären Ansatz, um außergewöhnliche Räume zu schaffen, die die Schönheit und Funktionalität des mediterranen und zeitlosen Stils widerspiegeln.

Basé à Palma et Portopetro, Ginard Luethje Wolf est une équipe créative germano-majorquine spécialisée en architecture et design d'intérieur. Leur approche se distingue par une esthétique visuellement claire et harmonieuse sans excès ornementaux. Avec une expérience locale étendue, l'équipe garantit la connexion entre le concept et l'exécution de chaque projet, des nouvelles urbanisations aux rénovations complètes. L'équipe est composée de Sebastià Ginard Adrover, architecte avec expérience internationale ; Lars Lüthje, expert en design d'intérieur et éclairage ; et Nina Wolf, designer spécialisée en couleur. Ensemble, ils offrent une approche multidisciplinaire pour créer des espaces exceptionnels reflétant la beauté et la fonctionnalité du style méditerranéen et intemporel.

Con sede en Palma y Portopetro, Ginard Luethje Wolf, es un equipo creativo germano-mallorquín especializado en arquitectura e interiorismo. Su enfoque se distingue por una estética visualmente clara y armoniosa, sin excesos ornamentales. Con una sólida experiencia local, el equipo garantiza la conexión entre el concepto y la ejecución de cada proyecto, desde urbanizaciones nuevas hasta renovaciones completas. El equipo está compuesto por Sebastià Ginard Adrover, arquitecto con experiencia internacional; Lars Lüthje, experto en diseño interior e iluminación; y Nina Wolf, diseñadora especializada en color. Juntos, ofrecen un enfoque multidisciplinario para crear espacios excepcionales que reflejan la belleza y la funcionalidad del estilo mediterráneo y atemporal.

PUENTE MILVIO PALMA CITY

ICAZAR
ARCHITECTS

CEO: ANDO SCHIRMER
HEAD OF DESIGN:
JOHANNES KIEFER

MALLORCA, SPAIN
ICAZAR.COM

Led by Ando Schirmer, Icazar combines traditional Mallorcan style and Mediterranean architecture with contemporary living. Their work aims at responsible construction using regional materials and short-distance logistics, minimizing environmental impact. From countryside houses to city apartments and hotels, their commitment to quality is reflected in the use of first-class materials and collaboration with local artisans who meet world-class standards to support the local economy and preserve ancestral crafts. Each project is a comprehensive experience for the client, guaranteeing satisfaction and high-end, custom-made products.

Geleitet von Ando Schirmer, kombiniert Icazar traditionellen mallorquinischen Stil und mediterrane Architektur mit zeitgenössischem Wohnen. Ihre Arbeit zielt auf verantwortungsbewusstes Bauen unter Verwendung regionaler Materialien und kurzer Logistikwege ab, um die Umweltbelastung zu minimieren. Von Landhäusern bis hin zu Stadtwohnungen und Hotels spiegelt ihr Engagement für Qualität sich in der Verwendung erstklassiger Materialien und der Zusammenarbeit mit lokalen Handwerkern wider, die Weltklasse-Standards erfüllen, um die lokale Wirtschaft zu unterstützen und traditionelles Handwerk zu bewahren. Jedes Projekt ist ein umfassendes Erlebnis für den Kunden und garantiert Zufriedenheit und maßgeschneiderte High-End-Produkte.

Dirigée par Ando Schirmer, Icazar combine le style traditionnel majorquin et l'architecture méditerranéenne avec un mode de vie contemporain. Leur travail vise une construction responsable utilisant des matériaux régionaux et une logistique à courte distance, minimisant l'impact environnemental. Des maisons de campagne aux appartements en ville et hôtels, leur engagement envers la qualité se reflète dans l'utilisation de matériaux de première classe et la collaboration avec des artisans locaux qui répondent aux normes de classe mondiale pour soutenir l'économie locale et préserver les métiers ancestraux. Chaque projet est une expérience intégrale pour le client, garantissant satisfaction et produits haut de gamme sur mesure.

Dirigido por Ando Schirmer, Icazar combina el estilo tradicional mallorquín y la arquitectura mediterránea con una forma de vida contemporánea. Su trabajo apunta a la construcción responsable, utilizando materiales regionales y logística de corta distancia, y minimizando el impacto ambiental. Desde casas en el campo hasta apartamentos en la ciudad y hoteles, su compromiso con la calidad se refleja en el uso de materiales de primera clase y la colaboración con artesanos locales que cumplen con estándares de clase mundial, para apoyar la economía local y preservar los oficios ancestrales. Cada proyecto es una experiencia integral para el cliente, garantizando satisfacción y productos de alta gama hechos a medida.

P. 80

CASA MARIPOSA

L D F L   S T U D I O

L U I S   D A V I D   F E R N Á N D E Z   L A O

MALLORCA, SPAIN
LDFLSTUDIO.COM

Architect Luis David Fernández Lao established LDFLstudio in 2017 after an extensive professional career in several countries, including the UK, Italy, and Spain. Settling in Mallorca, he was captivated by the island's beauty and architectural possibilities. He formed a multidisciplinary team to tackle projects that encompass landscape, architecture, and interior design. The combination of his international experiences with local architecture has resulted in pure, elegant, and functional designs. LDFLstudio focuses on evoking emotions through spaces that reflect the essence of the environment and meet the needs of their inhabitants.

Architekt Luis David Fernández Lao gründete LDFLstudio 2017 nach einer langen beruflichen Laufbahn in mehreren Ländern, darunter Großbritannien, Italien und Spanien. Als er sich auf Mallorca niederließ, war er von der Schönheit der Insel und ihren architektonischen Möglichkeiten fasziniert. Er bildete ein multidisziplinäres Team, um Projekte anzugehen, die Landschaft, Architektur und Innendesign umfassen. Die Kombination seiner internationalen Erfahrungen mit lokaler Architektur führte zu reinen, eleganten und funktionalen Designs. LDFLstudio konzentriert sich darauf, Emotionen durch Räume zu wecken, die das Wesen der Umgebung widerspiegeln und den Bedürfnissen ihrer Bewohner entsprechen.

L'architecte Luis David Fernández Lao a établi LDFLstudio en 2017 après une longue carrière professionnelle dans plusieurs pays, dont le Royaume-Uni, l'Italie et l'Espagne. S'installant à Majorque, il a été captivé par la beauté de l'île et ses possibilités architecturales. Il a formé une équipe multidisciplinaire pour aborder des projets englobant le paysage, l'architecture et le design intérieur. La combinaison de ses expériences internationales avec l'architecture locale a donné lieu à des designs purs, élégants et fonctionnels. LDFLstudio se concentre sur l'émotion des gens à travers des espaces reflétant l'essence de l'environnement et répondant aux besoins de leurs habitants.

El arquitecto Luis David Fernández Lao estableció LDFLstudio en 2017, tras una extensa carrera profesional en varios países como Reino Unido, Italia y España. Al asentarse en Mallorca, quedó cautivado por la belleza de la isla y sus posibilidades arquitectónicas. Formó un equipo multidisciplinar para abordar proyectos que abarcan el paisaje, la arquitectura y el diseño de interiores. La combinación de sus experiencias internacionales con la arquitectura local ha dado lugar a diseños puros, elegantes y funcionales. El enfoque de LDFLstudio se centra en emocionar a las personas a través de espacios que reflejan la esencia del entorno y satisfacen las necesidades de sus habitantes.

P. 90

CAN SERRA

LERYCKEMARTI
DESIGN

LAURA LERYCKE
JOAN MARTÍ

MALLORCA, SPAIN
LERYCKEMARTIDESIGN.COM

Founded by Laura Lerycke and Joan Martí, Lerycke Martí Design Studio specializes in interior design and decoration. Their approach is based on the proportion between environment, space, and client values present in every project. During the process, detailed analysis is prioritized, considering the location of the space, and the specific needs of each client. This approach, combined with precise diagnostics and the fusion of tradition and contemporaneity, guarantees effective accompaniment in each project, whether rehabilitation or new construction.

Gegründet von Laura Lerycke und Joan Martí, spezialisiert sich Lerycke Martí Design Studio auf Innendesign und Dekoration. Ihr Ansatz basiert auf dem Verhältnis zwischen Umwelt, Raum und den Werten des Kunden, die in jedem Projekt präsent sind. Während des Prozesses wird eine detaillierte Analyse durchgeführt, bei der die Lage des Raums und die spezifischen Bedürfnisse jedes Kunden berücksichtigt werden. Dieser Ansatz, kombiniert mit präzisen Diagnosen und der Verschmelzung von Tradition und Zeitgenossenschaft, gewährleistet eine effektive Begleitung in jedem Projekt, sei es bei der Sanierung oder beim Neubau.

Fondé par Laura Lerycke et Joan Martí, Lerycke Martí Design Estudio se spécialise en design d'intérieur et décoration. Leur approche repose sur la proportion entre l'environnement, l'espace et les valeurs du client présentes dans chaque projet. Lors du processus, une analyse détaillée est priorisée, en tenant compte de l'emplacement de l'espace, et des besoins spécifiques de chaque client. Cette approche, combinée à des diagnostics précis et à la fusion de la tradition et de la contemporanéité, garantit un accompagnement efficace dans chaque projet, qu'il s'agisse de réhabilitation ou de nouvelle construction.

Fundado por Laura Lerycke y Joan Martí, Lerycke Martí Design Estudio, se especializa en interiorismo y decoración. Su enfoque se basa en la proporción entre entorno, espacio y cliente, valores presentes en cada proyecto. Durante el proceso, se prioriza el análisis detallado, considerando la ubicación del espacio, así como las necesidades específicas de cada cliente. Este enfoque, combinado con un diagnóstico preciso y la fusión de tradición y contemporaneidad, garantiza un acompañamiento efectivo en cada proyecto, ya sea rehabilitación u obra nueva.

CAN PATRÓ

L F 9 1   D E S I G N
C O N S U L T A N T S

M I Q U E L   B A U Z Á

MALLORCA, SPAIN
LF91.COM

Established in 2006, LF91 focuses on residential and investment projects in Mallorca under the direction of Miquel Bauzá. With a trajectory that includes over 200 projects from country house or estate renovations to house and apartment remodels, the company seeks to harmoniously integrate its developments into the Mallorcan environment, respecting its culture and traditions. Their multidisciplinary team offers construction management services, encompassing everything from planning to final delivery. LF91 handles all administrative and financial aspects of the project, whether new constructions or renovations.

Gegründet 2006, konzentriert sich LF91 auf die Durchführung von Wohn- und Investitionsprojekten auf Mallorca unter der Leitung von Miquel Bauzá. Mit einer Laufbahn, die über 200 Projekte umfasst, von der Renovierung von Landhäusern oder Anwesen bis hin zu Haus- und Wohnungsrenovierungen, strebt das Unternehmen danach, seine Entwicklungen harmonisch in die mallorquinische Umgebung zu integrieren und respektiert dabei Kultur und Traditionen. Ihr multidisziplinäres Team bietet Baudienstleistungen an, die alles von der Planung bis zur endgültigen Lieferung umfassen. LF91 kümmert sich um alle administrativen und finanziellen Aspekte des Projekts, sei es bei Neubauten oder Renovierungen.

Fondée en 2006, LF91 se concentre sur la réalisation de projets résidentiels et d'investissement à Majorque sous la direction de Miquel Bauzá. Avec une trajectoire comprenant plus de 200 projets, des rénovations de maisons de campagne ou de domaines à la rénovation de maisons et d'appartements, l'entreprise cherche à intégrer harmonieusement ses développements dans l'environnement majorquin, en respectant sa culture et ses traditions. Leur équipe pluridisciplinaire offre des services de gestion de la construction, englobant tout, de la planification à la livraison finale. LF91 s'occupe de tous les aspects administratifs et financiers du projet, qu'il s'agisse de nouvelles constructions ou de rénovations.

Establecida en 2006, la firma LF91 se enfoca en la realización de proyectos residenciales y de inversión en Mallorca bajo la dirección de Miquel Bauzá. Con una trayectoria que incluye más de 200 proyectos, desde renovaciones de casas de campo o fincas, hasta la remodelación de viviendas y apartamentos, la empresa busca integrar sus desarrollos de manera armónica en el entorno mallorquín, respetando su cultura y tradiciones. Su equipo multidisciplinario ofrece servicios de gestión de construcción que abarcan desde la planificación hasta la entrega final. LF91 se encarga de todos los aspectos administrativos y financieros del proyecto, ya sean obras nuevas o reformas.

P. 112

CASA H

MARIA RAMIS
ARCHITECTURE

MARÍA RAMIS

MALLORCA, SPAIN
MARIARAMIS.COM

Maria Ramis is the founding architect of MR Architecture, a firm with over a decade of experience. Her approach is based on three pillars: light, Mediterranean design, and space functionality. Her works seek to maximize luminosity to bring spaces to life with modern design and respect for indigenous materials. Graduated with honors from ETSAB in Barcelona and specialized in Urban Appraisals at UPF, her career spans national and international projects. To carry out her vision, the architect has a team of professionals who share her great passion for architecture.

Maria Ramis ist die Gründerin von MR Architecture, einem Unternehmen mit über einem Jahrzehnt Erfahrung. Ihr Ansatz basiert auf drei Säulen: Licht, mediterranes Design und Raumfunktionalität. Ihre Werke zielen darauf ab, die Helligkeit zu maximieren, um Räume mit modernem Design und Respekt vor einheimischen Materialien zu beleben. Sie absolvierte mit Auszeichnung an der ETSAB in Barcelona und spezialisierte sich auf Stadtbewertungen an der UPF. Ihre Karriere umfasst nationale und internationale Projekte. Um ihre Vision umzusetzen, arbeitet die Architektin mit einem Team von Fachleuten zusammen, die ihre große Leidenschaft für Architektur teilen.

Maria Ramis est l'architecte fondatrice de MR Architecture, une entreprise avec plus d'une décennie d'expérience. Son approche repose sur trois piliers : la lumière, le design méditerranéen et la fonctionnalité des espaces. Ses œuvres cherchent à maximiser la luminosité pour donner vie aux espaces avec un design moderne et respectueux des matériaux indigènes. Diplômée avec mention de l'ETSAB de Barcelone et spécialisée en évaluation urbaine à l'UPF, sa carrière s'étend à des projets nationaux et internationaux. Pour réaliser sa vision, l'architecte s'entoure d'une équipe de professionnels partageant sa grande passion pour l'architecture.

Maria Ramis, es la arquitecta fundadora de MR Architecture una firma con más de una década de experiencia. Su enfoque se basa en tres pilares: la luz, el diseño mediterráneo y la funcionalidad de los espacios. Sus trabajos buscan maximizar la luminosidad para dar vida a los espacios, con un diseño moderno y respetuoso con los materiales autóctonos. Licenciada con honores en la ETSAB de Barcelona y especializada en Valoraciones Urbanísticas en la UPF, su trayectoria abarca proyectos nacionales e internacionales. Para llevar a cabo su visión, la arquitecta cuenta con un equipo de profesionales que comparten su pasión mayúscula por la arquitectura.

P. 122

CALA CARBÓ

MORGAN
AND MORGAN

PILLE MORGAN
LEIGH MORGAN

MALLORCA, SPAIN
MORGAN-MORGAN.CO.UK

Founded by Leigh Morgan and Pille Morgan, Morgan and Morgan is dedicated to real estate development. The firm, with a long track record, offers a comprehensive service for property search, construction, renovation, and vacation home rental in Mallorca. Each project reflects their commitment to quality and distinctive style. "Luxury in simplicity" is their guiding principle. The internal team and network of qualified contractors and architects provide tailored solutions for home construction and renovation. Their selection includes luxurious villas, rural retreats, and residences in Pollença.

Gegründet von Leigh Morgan und Pille Morgan widmet sich Morgan and Morgan der Immobilienentwicklung. Das Unternehmen, mit einer langen Erfolgsbilanz, bietet einen umfassenden Service für die Immobiliensuche, den Bau, die Renovierung und die Ferienhausvermietung auf Mallorca. Jedes Projekt spiegelt ihr Engagement für Qualität und einen unverwechselbaren Stil wider. „Luxus in Einfachheit" ist ihr Leitprinzip. Das interne Team und das Netzwerk qualifizierter Auftragnehmer und Architekten bieten maßgeschneiderte Lösungen für den Bau und die Renovierung von Häusern. Ihre Auswahl umfasst luxuriöse Villen, ländliche Rückzugsorte und Residenzen in Pollença.

Fondée par Leigh Morgan et Pille Morgan, Morgan and Morgan se consacre au développement immobilier. L'entreprise, avec une longue expérience, offre un service complet de recherche de propriétés, construction, rénovation et location de maisons de vacances à Majorque. Chaque projet reflète leur engagement envers la qualité et le style distinctif. « Le luxe dans la simplicité » est leur principe directeur. L'équipe interne et le réseau d'entrepreneurs et d'architectes qualifiés fournissent des solutions adaptées pour la construction et la rénovation de maisons. Leur sélection comprend des villas luxueuses, des retraites rurales et des résidences à Pollença.

Fundada por Leigh Morgan y Pille Morgan, Morgan and Morgan se dedica al desarrollo inmobiliario. La firma ofrece que cuenta con una larga trayectoria ofrece un servicio integral de búsqueda de propiedades, construcción, renovación y alquiler de casas de vacaciones en Mallorca. Cada proyecto refleja su compromiso con la calidad y el estilo distintivos. «El lujo en la simplicidad» es su principio rector. El equipo interno y red de contratistas y arquitectos calificados brindan soluciones adaptadas para la construcción y renovación de viviendas. Su selección incluye villas lujosas, retiros rurales y residencias en Pollença.

P. 132

SON PI FINCA BREEZE

MY LANDSCAPING GROUP

JOHANNES DÜTSCH

MALLORCA, SPAIN
MYLANDSCAPINGGROUP.COM

Johannes Dütsch founded My Landscaping Group in 2014 in Mallorca. With extensive experience in designing Mediterranean gardens, the team consists of landscape architects, draftsmen, and graphic designers who collaborate with engineers, botanists, surveyors, and gardeners. This synergy allows for professional planning and management of even the most demanding and extensive gardens. After working in Munich and the south of France, Dütsch settled in Mallorca in 2008. For six years, he collaborated with Jardins de Tramuntana before becoming independent with the creation of his landscaping company in Santa Ponsa.

Johannes Dütsch gründete My Landscaping Group 2014 auf Mallorca. Mit umfangreicher Erfahrung in der Gestaltung mediterraner Gärten besteht das Team aus Landschaftsarchitekten, Zeichnern und Grafikdesignern, die mit Ingenieuren, Botanikern, Vermessungsingenieuren und Gärtnern zusammenarbeiten. Diese Synergie ermöglicht die professionelle Planung und Verwaltung selbst der anspruchsvollsten und umfangreichsten Gärten. Nach seiner Arbeit in München und Südfrankreich ließ sich Dütsch 2008 auf Mallorca nieder. Er arbeitete sechs Jahre lang bei Jardins de Tramuntana, bevor er in Santa Ponsa sein eigenes Landschaftsbauunternehmen gründete.

Johannes Dütsch a fondé My Landscaping Group en 2014 à Majorque. Avec une vaste expérience dans la conception de jardins méditerranéens, l'équipe se compose d'architectes paysagistes, de dessinateurs et de designers graphiques qui collaborent avec des ingénieurs, des botanistes, des topographes et des jardiniers. Cette synergie permet de planifier et de gérer professionnellement même les jardins les plus exigeants et les plus étendus. Après avoir travaillé à Munich et dans le sud de la France, Dütsch s'est installé à Majorque en 2008. Pendant six ans, il a collaboré avec Jardins de Tramuntana avant de devenir indépendant avec la création de son atelier d'aménagement paysager à Santa Ponsa.

Johannes Dütsch fundó en 2014 el estudio de paisajismo My Landscaping Group en Mallorca. Con una amplia experiencia en el diseño de jardines mediterráneos, el equipo se compone de arquitectos paisajistas, delineantes y diseñadores gráficos, quienes colaboran con ingenieros, botánicos, topógrafos y jardineros. Esta sinergia permite planificar y gestionar profesionalmente hasta los jardines más exigentes y extensos. Tras su experiencia laboral en Múnich y el sur de Francia, Dütsch se instaló en Mallorca en 2008. Durante seis años colaboró con Jardins de Tramuntana, antes de independizarse con la creación de su estudio de paisajismo en Santa Ponsa.

P. 144

CAN SANTACILIA

Photo: © Ben Roberts

O H L A B

P A L O M A   H E R N A I Z
J A I M E   O L I V E R

PALMA DE MALLORCA, MADRID, NEW YORK
OHLAB.NET

OHLAB is an office dedicated to urban analysis and cultural research of contemporary society through design, architectural practice, and urban strategy. Led by Paloma Hernaiz and Jaime Oliver, the firm has received significant recognition, such as the double nomination for the Mies van der Rohe Award and the 2022 Architecture Masterprize award for Best Architecture Firm of the Year. Internationally renowned for its excellence in design and sustainability, OHLAB works on residential, hotel, and commercial projects. The office, founded in 2007 in Shanghai and now located in Palma de Mallorca, has a team of professionals committed to innovation and architectural quality.

OHLAB ist ein Büro, das sich der urbanen Analyse und kulturellen Erforschung der zeitgenössischen Gesellschaft durch Design, architektonische Praxis und urbane Strategie widmet. Unter der Leitung von Paloma Hernaiz und Jaime Oliver hat das Unternehmen bedeutende Anerkennungen erhalten, wie die doppelte Nominierung für den Mies van der Rohe Preis und den 2022 Architecture Masterprize Award für das beste Architekturbüro des Jahres. International anerkannt für seine Exzellenz im Design und in der Nachhaltigkeit, arbeitet OHLAB an Wohn-, Hotel- und Gewerbeprojekten. Das Büro wurde 2007 in Shanghai gegründet und hat jetzt seinen Sitz in Palma de Mallorca, mit einem Team von Fachleuten, die sich der Innovation und architektonischen Qualität verschrieben haben.

OHLAB est un bureau dédié à l'analyse urbaine et à la recherche culturelle de la société contemporaine à travers le design, la pratique architecturale et la stratégie urbaine. Dirigée par Paloma Hernaiz et Jaime Oliver, l'entreprise a reçu d'importantes reconnaissances, telles que la double nomination pour le prix Mies van der Rohe et le prix 2022 Architecture Masterprize de la meilleure entreprise d'architecture de l'année. Reconnu internationalement pour son excellence en design et durabilité, OHLAB travaille sur des projets résidentiels, hôteliers et commerciaux. Le bureau, fondé en 2007 à Shanghai et maintenant situé à Palma de Majorque, compte une équipe de professionnels engagés dans l'innovation et la qualité architecturale.

OHLAB es una oficina dedicada al análisis urbano y la investigación cultural de la sociedad contemporánea a través del diseño, la práctica arquitectónica y la estrategia urbana. Liderada por Paloma Hernaiz y Jaime Oliver, la firma ha recibido importantes reconocimientos, como la doble nominación al Premio Mies van der Rohe y el premio a la Mejor Firma de Arquitectura del Año por Architecture Masterprize en 2022. Destacada internacionalmente por su excelencia en diseño y sostenibilidad, OHLAB trabaja en proyectos residenciales, hoteleros y comerciales. La oficina, fundada en 2007 en Shanghai y ahora ubicada en Palma de Mallorca, cuenta con un equipo de profesionales comprometidos con la innovación y la calidad arquitectónica.

P. 152

VERDEROL

PORTELL   DESIGN
&   CONSTRUCTION

INÉS   PORTELL
ANTONIO   PORTELL

MALLORCA, SPAIN
PORTELL-PORTELL.COM

Led by Inés and Antonio Portell, Portell Design & Construction excels in the design and construction sector. Inés, an interior design specialist trained at ESDIB with additional studies in London and Milan, focuses on high-end residential and commercial projects, as well as participating in teaching. Antonio, the third generation of master builders, trained in advanced construction techniques, has taken the family business beyond its 50-year legacy, integrating new technologies and sustainable practices into projects ranging from the rehabilitation of historic palaces to renovations in Andratx. Together, they maintain a commitment to quality and innovation, providing services that meet the contemporary demands of their clients.

Unter der Leitung von Inés und Antonio Portell zeichnet sich Portell Design & Construction im Bereich Design und Bau aus. Inés, eine auf Innendesign spezialisierte Fachkraft, die an der ESDIB ausgebildet wurde und zusätzliche Studien in London und Mailand absolviert hat, konzentriert sich auf hochwertige Wohn- und Gewerbeprojekte und beteiligt sich zudem an der Lehre. Antonio, dritte Generation von Baumeistern und in fortschrittlichen Bautechniken ausgebildet, hat das Familienunternehmen über sein 50-jähriges Erbe hinausgeführt und neue Technologien und nachhaltige Praktiken in Projekte integriert, die von der Sanierung historischer Paläste bis hin zu Renovierungen in Andratx reichen. Gemeinsam setzen sie sich für Qualität und Innovation ein und bieten Dienstleistungen an, die den zeitgenössischen Anforderungen ihrer Kunden gerecht werden.

Dirigée par Inés et Antonio Portell, Portell Design & Construction se distingue dans le secteur du design et de la construction. Inés, spécialiste en design d'intérieur formée à l'ESDIB avec des études supplémentaires à Londres et à Milan, se concentre sur des projets commerciaux et résidentiels haut de gamme, en plus de participer à l'enseignement. Antonio, troisième génération de maîtres d'œuvre et formé aux techniques de construction avancées, a conduit l'entreprise familiale au-delà de son héritage de 50 ans, intégrant de nouvelles technologies et des pratiques durables dans des projets allant de la réhabilitation de palais historiques à des rénovations à Andratx. Ensemble, ils maintiennent un engagement envers la qualité et l'innovation, offrant des services qui répondent aux exigences contemporaines de leurs clients.

Dirigido por Inés y Antonio Portell, Portell Design & Construction destaca en el sector del diseño y construcción. Inés, especialista en interiorismo formada en ESDIB y con estudios adicionales en Londres y Milán, se concentra en proyectos comerciales y de viviendas de alto standing, además de participar en la docencia. Antonio, tercera generación de maestros de obra y formado en técnicas constructivas avanzadas, ha llevado la empresa familiar más allá de su legado de 50 años, integrando nuevas tecnologías y prácticas sostenibles en proyectos que van desde la rehabilitación de palacetes históricos hasta reformas en Andratx. Juntos, mantienen un compromiso con la calidad y la innovación, ofreciendo servicios que cumplen con las demandas contemporáneas de sus clientes.

P. 164

SANTANYÍ

P S A R Q U I T E C T O S
+ M A R G A C O M A S
I N T E R I O R D E S I G N

P E D R O D E S A L V A D O R
M O R E L L
M A R G A C O M A S

MALLORCA, SPAIN
PSARQUITECTOS.ES | MARGACOMAS.COM

PS Arquitectos is the firm of Pedro de Salvador Morell, an architect with postgraduate degrees in urban planning, land management, and project management. With extensive experience in architecture, interior design, and construction management services, the studio specializes in the design of single-family housing in Mallorca.
Marga Comas is an interior designer trained in Barcelona and Oslo with extensive experience in designing hotels in the Caribbean. Since her return in 2010, she developed numerous interior design and decoration projects, and found her own studio.

PS Arquitectos ist die Firma von Pedro de Salvador Morell, einem Architekten mit Postgraduiertenabschlüssen in Stadtplanung, Raumordnung und Projektmanagement. Mit umfassender Erfahrung in den Bereichen Architektur, Innenarchitektur und Baumanagement spezialisiert sich das Studio auf das Design von Einfamilienhäusern auf Mallorca.
Marga Comas ist eine Innendesignerin, die in Barcelona und Oslo ausgebildet wurde und umfangreiche Erfahrung in der Gestaltung von Hotels in der Karibik hat. Seit ihrer Rückkehr im Jahr 2010 hat sie zahlreiche Innenarchitektur- und Dekorationsprojekte entwickelt und ihr eigenes Studio gegründet.

PS Arquitectos est le cabinet de Pedro de Salvador Morell, un architecte avec des diplômes de troisième cycle en droit de l'urbanisme et aménagement du territoire. Avec une vaste expérience en architecture, design d'intérieur et services de gestion de la construction, le studio se spécialise en la conception de logements unifamiliaux à Majorque.
Marga Comas est une designer d'intérieur formée à Barcelone et Oslo avec une vaste expérience dans la conception d'hôtels dans les Caraïbes. Depuis son retour en 2010, elle a développé de nombreux projets de design d'intérieur et de décoration, et a fondé son propre studio.

PS Arquitectos es la firma de Pedro de Salvador Morell, un arquitecto con posgrados en Derecho Urbanístico y Ordenación del territorio, y en Project Management. Con una vasta experiencia en servicios de arquitectura, diseño de interiores y gestión de obras, el estudio se especializa en el diseño de vivienda unifamiliar en Mallorca.
Marga Comas es una interiorista con formación en Barcelona y Oslo, que cuenta con una extensa experiencia en el diseño de hoteles en el Caribe. Desde su regreso en 2010, desarrolló numerosos proyectos de diseño de interiores y decoración, y fundó su propio estudio.

P. 174

HOTEL SON BUNYOLA

RIALTO LIVING
INTERIOR DESIGN
STUDIO

MALLORCA, SPAIN
RIALTOLIVING.COM

Rialto Living is a Lifestyle store and interior design studio in Mallorca. Their team of designers, whose motto is "relaxed elegance" experts in Mediterranean timeless style, offers high-quality furniture and fabrics to create personalized spaces tailored to their clients' needs. From rustic properties to contemporary ones, the firm led by Klas Kall and Barbara Bergman has collaborated on the interiors of Mallorca's most exclusive properties. Founded in 2007, Rialto Living transformed the old Rialto Theater into a vibrant concept store. In 2014, renovated the whole building, Can O'Ryan, and doubled their space in a building where they restored the original Baroque elements to expand their range of products and sections.

Rialto Living ist ein Lifestyle-Geschäft und Innenarchitektur-Studio auf Mallorca. Das Team von Designern, deren Motto „entspannte Eleganz" lautet und die Experten für den zeitlosen mediterranen Stil sind, bietet hochwertige Möbel und Stoffe an, um individuelle Räume zu schaffen, die auf die Bedürfnisse ihrer Kunden zugeschnitten sind. Das von Klas Kall und Barbara Bergman geleitete Büro hat an der Inneneinrichtung der exklusivsten Immobilien Mallorcas mitgewirkt, von rustikalen bis hin zu modernen Objekten. Das 2007 gegründete Unternehmen Rialto Living verwandelte das alte Rialto-Theater in einen lebendigen Concept Store. Im Jahr 2014 renovierten sie das gesamte Gebäude Can O'Ryan und verdoppelten ihre Fläche in einem Gebäude, in dem sie die ursprünglichen Barockelemente restaurierten, um ihr Angebot an Produkten und Abteilungen zu erweitern.

Rialto Living est un magasin de référence et un studio de design d'intérieur à Majorque. Leur équipe de designers, experts en style majorquin, propose des meubles et des tissus de haute qualité pour créer des espaces personnalisés adaptés aux besoins de leurs clients. Des propriétés rustiques aux contemporaines, l'entreprise dirigée par Klas Kall et Barbara Bergman a collaboré sur les intérieurs des propriétés les plus exclusives de Majorque. Fondée en 2007, Rialto Living a transformé l'ancien théâtre Rialto en un concept-store vibrant. En 2014, ils ont rénové l'ensemble du bâtiment Can O'Ryan et doublé leur espace dans un bâtiment dont ils ont restauré les éléments baroques d'origine afin d'élargir leur gamme de produits et de sections.

Rialto Living es un estudio de diseño de interiores y lifestyle store de referencia en Mallorca. Su equipo de diseñadores crean espacios en un estilo mediterráneo atemporal, y ofrecen mobiliario y telas de alta calidad para crear ambientes personalizados, adaptándose a las necesidades de sus clientes. Desde propiedades rústicas hasta contemporáneas, la firma, liderada por Klas Kall y Barbara Bergman, ha colaborado en los interiores de las propiedades más exclusivas de Mallorca. Fundada en 2007, Rialto Living transformó el antiguo teatro Rialto en un concept-store vibrante. En 2014, adquiere y reforma todo el edificio a Can O'Ryan, y duplica su superficie con una propiedad en la que ha restaurado los elementos barrocos originales para expandir su gama de productos y secciones.

P. 184

CASA MARGARITA

RÔCK & VILLA

STEFAN RELIC
PAULO VALCIC

MALLORCA, SPAIN
ROCKANDVILLA.COM

Led by Paulo Valcic and Stefan Relic, the real estate development firm Rôck&Villa specializes in restoring traditional Mallorcan houses. Their meticulous approach preserves heritage while incorporating high-quality finishes, blending history and modernity.

Paulo, an architect and interior designer with over 20 years of experience, is the project manager. From conception to completion, he supervises every stage and takes on creative direction. Stefan, a digital professional with a passion for interior design and real estate, collaborates in property search, financial planning, and marketing strategy.

Geleitet von Paulo Valcic und Stefan Relic, spezialisiert sich das Immobilienentwicklungsunternehmen Rôck&Villa auf die Restaurierung traditioneller mallorquinischer Häuser. Ihr akribischer Ansatz bewahrt das Erbe und integriert gleichzeitig hochwertige Oberflächen, die Geschichte und Moderne miteinander verbinden.

Paulo, Architekt und Innenarchitekt mit über 20 Jahren Erfahrung, ist Projektleiter. Von der Konzeption bis zur Fertigstellung überwacht er jede Phase und übernimmt die kreative Leitung. Stefan, ein Digitalprofi mit einer Leidenschaft für Innendesign und Immobilien, arbeitet an der Immobiliensuche, Finanzplanung und Marketingstrategie.

Dirigée par Paulo Valcic et Stefan Relic, l'entreprise de développement immobilier Rôck&Villa se spécialise dans la restauration de maisons traditionnelles majorquines. Leur approche méticuleuse préserve le patrimoine tout en incorporant des finitions de haute qualité, fusionnant histoire et modernité.

Paulo, architecte et designer d'intérieur avec plus de 20 ans d'expérience, est le gestionnaire de projet. De la conception à la réalisation, il supervise chaque étape et assume la direction créative. Stefan, professionnel du numérique passionné par le design d'intérieur et l'immobilier, collabore à la recherche de propriétés, à la planification financière et à la stratégie marketing.

Liderado por Paulo Valcic y Stefan Relic, la firma de desarrollo inmobiliario Rôck&Villa, se especializa en la restauración de casas tradicionales mallorquinas. Su enfoque meticuloso preserva el patrimonio mientras incorpora acabados de alta calidad, fusionando historia y modernidad.

Paulo, arquitecto y diseñador de interiores con más de 20 años de experiencia, es el gestor de proyectos. Desde la concepción hasta la finalización, supervisa cada etapa y asume la dirección creativa. Stefan, profesional digital con pasión por el diseño de interiores y bienes raíces, colabora en la búsqueda de propiedades, planificación financiera y estrategia de marketing.

P. 196

CASA DE CAMPO

SOLÍS
BETANCOURT
& SHERRILL

JOSÉ SOLÍS
PAUL SHERRILL

WASHINGTON DC, UNITED STATES OF AMERICA
SOLISBETANCOURT.COM

Since its founding in 1990, Solís Betancourt & Sherrill has established itself as a leading residential design firm, gaining international recognition. Their projects have been featured in prestigious publications such as Architectural Digest, Traditional Home, House Beautiful, The New York Times Magazine, and The Washington Post. In 2010, Monacelli Press published their monograph "Essential Elegance," a compendium of their work. For José Solís and Paul Sherrill, partners at Solís Betancourt & Sherrill, the goal of each interior is to achieve a balance between formal and informal, traditional and contemporary, never forgetting comfort and livability. Their designs transcend daily routine, offering spaces of elegance, tranquility, and beauty, making each room a cozy sanctuary.

Seit seiner Gründung im Jahr 1990 hat sich Solís Betancourt & Sherrill als führendes Unternehmen im Wohnungsdesign etabliert und internationale Anerkennung erlangt. Ihre Projekte wurden in angesehenen Publikationen wie Architectural Digest, Traditional Home, House Beautiful, The New York Times Magazine und The Washington Post vorgestellt. Im Jahr 2010 veröffentlichte Monacelli Press ihre Monographie „Essential Elegance", eine Sammlung ihrer Arbeiten. Für José Solís und Paul Sherrill, Partner bei Solís Betancourt & Sherrill, ist das Ziel jedes Innenraums, ein Gleichgewicht zwischen formal und informell, traditionell und zeitgenössisch zu erreichen, ohne dabei Komfort und Lebensqualität zu vergessen. Ihre Designs gehen über den täglichen Alltag hinaus und bieten Räume von Eleganz, Ruhe und Schönheit, die jeden Raum zu einem gemütlichen Zufluchtsort machen.

Depuis sa fondation en 1990, Solís Betancourt & Sherrill s'est imposé comme une entreprise leader en design résidentiel, obtenant une reconnaissance internationale. Leurs projets ont été présentés dans des publications prestigieuses telles que Architectural Digest, Traditional Home, House Beautiful, The New York Times Magazine et The Washington Post. En 2010, Monacelli Press a publié leur monographie « Essential Elegance », un recueil de leur travail. Pour José Solís et Paul Sherrill, partenaires chez Solís Betancourt & Sherrill, l'objectif de chaque intérieur est d'atteindre un équilibre entre le formel et l'informel, le traditionnel et le contemporain, sans jamais oublier le confort et l'habitabilité. Leurs designs transcendent la routine quotidienne, offrant des espaces d'élégance, de tranquillité et de beauté, faisant de chaque pièce un sanctuaire accueillant.

Desde su fundación en 1990, Solís Betancourt & Sherrill se ha consolidado como una firma líder en diseño residencial, obteniendo reconocimiento internacional. Sus proyectos han sido destacados en publicaciones de prestigio como Architectural Digest, Traditional Home, House Beautiful, The New York Times Magazine y The Washington Post. En 2010, Monacelli Press publicó su monografía «Essential Elegance», un compendio de su trabajo. Para José Solís y Paul Sherrill, socios de Solís Betancourt & Sherrill, el objetivo de cada interior es lograr un equilibrio entre lo formal y lo informal, lo tradicional y lo contemporáneo, sin olvidar nunca la comodidad y la habitabilidad. Sus diseños trascienden la rutina diaria, ofreciendo espacios de elegancia, tranquilidad y belleza, convirtiendo cada habitación en un santuario acogedor.

P. 206

CBF HOUSE

TARRAGONA-HÖHNE ARQUITECTOS + JORGE BIBILONI STUDIO

ANNA TARRAGONA
LARS HÖHNE
JORGE BIBILONI

MALLORCA, SPAIN
TH-A.COM | JORGEBIBILONISTUDIO.COM

Founded in 2002 by Anna Tarragona and Lars Höhne, this architecture studio combines Mediterranean warmth with German efficiency and functionality. Tarragona Höhne Architects is distinguished by offering personalized architecture and comprehensive services with a specialization in high-end residences. Their focus is on contemporary luxury characterized by timeless elegance and quality. On the other hand, after extensive experience in international interior design firms, Jorge Bibiloni has his interior design studio in Palma de Mallorca. The studio is based on attention to detail and a sensitive selection of materials. Their designs are characterized by purity, elegance, and functionality. In 2013, he co-founded Domun, offering comprehensive services from design to execution.

Gegründet 2002 von Anna Tarragona und Lars Höhne, kombiniert dieses Architekturbüro mediterrane Wärme mit deutscher Effizienz und Funktionalität. Tarragona Höhne Architects zeichnet sich durch die Bereitstellung personalisierter Architektur und umfassender Dienstleistungen aus, mit einer Spezialisierung auf hochwertige Residenzen. Ihr Fokus liegt auf zeitgemäßem Luxus, der durch zeitlose Eleganz und Qualität gekennzeichnet ist. Auf der anderen Seite hat Jorge Bibiloni nach umfangreicher Erfahrung in internationalen Innenarchitekturbüros sein eigenes Innenarchitekturstudio in Palma de Mallorca. Das Studio basiert auf der Liebe zum Detail und einer sensiblen Materialauswahl. Ihre Designs zeichnen sich durch Reinheit, Eleganz und Funktionalität aus. 2013 gründete er Domun mit, um umfassende Dienstleistungen von der Gestaltung bis zur Ausführung anzubieten.

Fondé en 2002 par Anna Tarragona et Lars Höhne, ce studio d'architecture combine la chaleur méditerranéenne avec l'efficacité et la fonctionnalité allemandes. Tarragona Höhne Architects se distingue par l'offre d'une architecture personnalisée et de services complets avec une spécialisation dans les résidences haut de gamme. Leur objectif est de créer un luxe contemporain caractérisé par une élégance intemporelle et une qualité. D'autre part, après une vaste expérience dans des cabinets internationaux de design d'intérieur, Jorge Bibiloni possède son studio de design d'intérieur à Palma de Majorque. Le studio est basé sur l'attention aux détails et une sélection sensible des matériaux. Leurs designs se caractérisent par la pureté, l'élégance et la fonctionnalité. En 2013, il a co-fondé Domun, offrant des services complets de la conception à l'exécution.

Fundado en 2002 por Anna Tarragona y Lars Höhne, este estudio de arquitectura fusiona la calidez mediterránea con la eficiencia y funcionalidad alemanas. Tarragona Höhne Architects se distingue por ofrecer arquitectura personalizada y servicios integrales, con especialización en residencias de alta gama. Su enfoque se centra en el lujo contemporáneo, caracterizado por la elegancia atemporal y la calidad. Por su parte, y tras una larga experiencia en firmas de interiorismo internacionales, Jorge Bibiloni, tiene su estudio de interiorismo en Palma de Mallorca. El estudio se fundamenta en el cuidado por el detalle y la selección sensible de materiales. Sus diseños se caracterizan por la pureza, elegancia y funcionalidad. En 2013, co-funda Domum, ofreciendo servicios integrales desde diseño hasta ejecución.

P. 216

CASA PASSARATX

THE EAZEY

SMILJANA KAISER-HOHENEDER
RAINER HOHENEDER

MALLORCA, SPAIN
THEEAZEY.COM

With extensive experience in the modeling and fashion design industry, Smiljana Kaiser-Hoheneder and Rainer Hoheneder have been in the world of aesthetics for decades. Once settled in Mallorca, they have focused on restoring estates and village houses. Their approach centers on preserving the traditional character of stone buildings, blending the old with the new. In interior design, they stand out for their simple elegance and use of natural materials, creating harmonious environments that reflect the Mediterranean lifestyle with a cosmopolitan touch.

Mit umfangreicher Erfahrung in der Model- und Modedesignbranche haben Smiljana Kaiser-Hoheneder und Rainer Hoheneder Jahrzehnte in der Welt der Ästhetik verbracht. Einmal auf Mallorca niedergelassen, konzentrierten sie sich auf die Restaurierung von Anwesen und Dorfhäusern. Ihr Ansatz zielt darauf ab, den traditionellen Charakter von Steingebäuden zu bewahren und das Alte mit dem Neuen zu verschmelzen. Im Innendesign zeichnen sie sich durch einfache Eleganz und die Verwendung natürlicher Materialien aus, wodurch harmonische Umgebungen entstehen, die den mediterranen Lebensstil mit einem kosmopolitischen Touch widerspiegeln.

Avec une vaste expérience dans l'industrie du mannequinat et du design de mode, Smiljana Kaiser-Hoheneder et Rainer Hoheneder ont évolué dans le monde de l'esthétique pendant des décennies. Une fois installés à Majorque, ils se sont orientés vers la restauration de propriétés et de maisons de village. Leur approche se concentre sur la préservation du caractère traditionnel des bâtiments en pierre, fusionnant l'ancien et le nouveau. En design intérieur, ils se distinguent par leur élégance simple et l'utilisation de matériaux naturels, créant des environnements harmonieux reflétant le style de vie méditerranéen avec une touche cosmopolite.

Con una amplia experiencia en la industria del modelaje y el diseño de moda, Smiljana Kaiser-Hoheneder y Rainer Hoheneder han transitado en el mundo de la estética por décadas. Una vez instalados en Mallorca se han orientado a la restauración de fincas y casas de pueblo. Su enfoque se centra en preservar el carácter tradicional de los edificios de piedra, fusionando lo antiguo con lo moderno. En diseño interior, destacan por su elegancia sencilla y el uso de materiales naturales, creando ambientes armoniosos que reflejan el estilo de vida mediterráneo con un toque cosmopolita.

P. 224

CASA DEL SINDICATO

T N W   D E S I G N

T H O M A S   N I E D E R S T E - W E R B E C K

MALLORCA, SPAIN
TNWDESIGN.COM

TNW Design was founded in 2016 by German designer Thomas Niederste-Werbeck. Trained in art history at Christie's Education London and former creative director and editor-in-chief of German magazines such as Architektur & Wohnen, Salon, and Häuser, Thomas is an interior designer and creative consultant. His passion lies in natural materials such as wood, handwoven baskets, bronze, earth, linen, and eroded stone. He prefers pure and tactile materials for clear and timeless design with warm tones that capture sunlight. His approach respects the authenticity and tradition of the place, resisting fashions and trends.

TNW Design wurde 2016 vom deutschen Designer Thomas Niederste-Werbeck gegründet. Ausgebildet in Kunstgeschichte an Christie's Education London und ehemaliger Kreativdirektor und Chefredakteur deutscher Magazine wie Architektur & Wohnen, Salon und Häuser, ist Thomas Innenarchitekt und Kreativberater. Seine Leidenschaft gilt natürlichen Materialien wie Holz, handgewebten Körben, Bronze, Erde, Leinen und erodiertem Stein. Er bevorzugt reine und taktile Materialien für ein klares und zeitloses Design mit warmen Tönen, die das Sonnenlicht einfangen. Sein Ansatz respektiert die Authentizität und Tradition des Ortes und widersteht Moden und Trends.

TNW Design a été fondé en 2016 par le designer allemand Thomas Niederste-Werbeck. Formé en histoire de l'art à Christie's Education Londres et ancien directeur créatif et rédacteur en chef de magazines allemands tels que Architektur & Wohnen, Salon et Häuser, Thomas est designer d'intérieur et consultant créatif. Sa passion réside dans les matériaux naturels comme le bois, les paniers tissés à la main, le bronze, la terre, le lin et la pierre érodée. Il préfère les matériaux purs et tactiles pour un design clair et intemporel avec des tons chauds capturant la lumière du soleil. Son approche respecte l'authenticité et la tradition du lieu, résistant aux modes et aux tendances.

TNW Design fue fundado en 2016 por el diseñador alemán Thomas Niederste-Werbeck. Formado en historia del arte en Christie's Education, Londres, y exdirector creativo y redactor jefe de revistas alemanas como Architektur & Wohnen, Salon y Häuser, Thomas es diseñador de interiores y consultor creativo. Su pasión reside en materiales naturales como la madera, cestas tejidas a mano, bronce, tierra, lino y piedra erosionada. Prefiere materiales puros y táctiles para un diseño claro y atemporal, con tonos cálidos que capturan la luz del sol. Su enfoque respeta la autenticidad y la tradición del lugar, resistiendo modas y tendencias.

Editorial project:
© 2024 **booq** publishing, S.L.
c/ Domènech, 7-9, 2º 1ª
08012 Barcelona, Spain
T: +34 93 268 80 88
www.booqpublishing.com

ISBN: 978-84-9936-616-6 [EN]
ISBN: 978-84-9936-605-0 [ES]

Editorial coordinator:
Claudia Martínez Alonso

Art director:
Mireia Casanovas Soley

Editor:
Daniela Santos Quartino

Layout:
Cristina Simó Perales

Translation:
© **booq** publishing, S.L.

Sketch Page 1:
LDFL Studio

Printing in China